COUNTRY MATTERS

DUFF HART-DAVIS

COUNTRY
MATTERS

Illustrations by George Tute

WEIDENFELD AND NICOLSON · LONDON

First published in Great Britain in 1988 by
George Weidenfeld & Nicolson Limited,
91 Clapham High Street, London SW4 7TA

Text copyright © Duff Hart-Davis 1986, 1987, 1988
Illustrations copyright © George Tute 1988

ISBN 0 297 79460 4

Printed and bound in Great Britain by
Butler & Tanner Ltd, Frome and London

Contents

Foreword

Whenever I see one of these pieces in print, I think uneasily of a remark made by that splendid poet and critic William Plomer. When asked what he thought of the latest offering from some romantic novelist, he replied that he found the book so light that he almost had to hold it down to read it.

So with these trifles. The fact that they exist at all is due largely to Andreas Whittam Smith, founder-editor of *The Independent*, who not only had the courage and skill to launch a new national newspaper in October 1986, but took another substantial risk in appointing me its Country Matters correspondent.

'So you're Boot of *The Independent*!' said friends with patronizing smiles. 'What sort of stuff are you going to write?' I could not be sure; all I could say for certain was that my column would not be about the questing vole, passing feather-footed through the plashy fen. I hoped it would be something more robust and earthy, something that gave a true reflection of life on the land.

I am often asked whether my Editor realizes that the title chosen for the column is a salacious quotation from Shakespeare. 'Of course,' I always reply; for he, being a civilized fellow, knows his *Hamlet* as well as anyone – and indeed one of the joys of writing for *The Independent* is that an author receives maximum intelligent support combined with minimal editorial interference.

JANUARY

No Christmas or New Year celebrations lit up the windows of the old house at the top of the hill. Unless ghosts came out to make merry, nobody stirred in its dank and dismal rooms, for the place has been standing empty since its last occupants departed eight months ago. Walking past it up the footpath at dusk on New Year's Eve, I found myself gripped by the image of Walter de la Mare's lone horseman who comes to the empty mansion in the forest:

'Is there anybody there?' said the traveller,
Knocking on the moonlit door...

Though not by any means beautiful, the house has a certain charm bred of age and irregularity; but for me its main attraction is that it occupies a marvellous site – a ten-acre plateau on the brow of the escarpment, tucked away above the beech woods (in which the winds roar), and commanding forty-mile views into the mountains of central Wales.

Rumour has it that in the spring the place was bought by a foreign businessman, but that his wife (or fiancée or girlfriend) took one look at it and made off at high speed, thus causing it to be put back on the market. If she did, I do not blame her, for there is no denying that the house and grounds have a melancholy air, intensified by the state of decay into which everything has fallen. The fruit trees are gnarled and misshapen, ivy has rioted over the garden walls, and the remains of a once elegant iron fence are rusting quietly away. Lured by the lack of disturbance, pheasants have drawn into the garden, and twice I have put a fox out of the shrubbery.

Clearly the last occupant had no time for plants or trees; but he was the most terrific magpie, and assembled ancient vehicles and engines as other people collect postage stamps. For years before his departure a dead motor boat had lain becalmed in the vegetable garden, and two decrepit old bangers had been visible in the open-fronted garage. Then, as he was about to leave, several further wrecks were dragged from the undergrowth, and defunct equipment was carted off by the skipful. Now there is no more than one car, a sink or two and the best part of a tractor, mouldering in a pit at the end of the field, to mark his passion.

Yet it is precisely the neglect that appeals so strongly to me. I wish the place to remain as it is, and I dread the moment when some new owner arrives to sort it out. Trying to analyse why this should be so, I come to the conclusion that attraction lies in the fact that the property offers such scope for improvement.

Whenever I walk past, I think through the innumerable things one would have to do to make it habitable: remodel the inside of the house, replace the windows, re-slate the roof, dig new drains, bulldoze bushes, plant new trees, get rid of the old iron railings (itself no small task), construct a ha-ha, fence and re-seed the field, clear out the pit, build new stables, re-establish the vegetable garden, massacre the ivy . . .

All this would go through £100,000 at least, on top of the £300,000 or so that the property would cost to buy. But since I am already comfortably housed and have no intention of buying, I can indulge my fantasies without the slightest risk to my pocket: I can plan away without any commitment or action. The longer the house remains empty, the more rein my imagination will have: the better I shall be able to sustain the illusion that the old building is inhabited only by de la Mare's phantom Listeners, and that I, as I come up out of the trees on winter evenings, am the one man left awake.

Rescued from oblivion

Last Sunday morning Mike Neville, a self-employed mechanic and keen shooting-man, drove over to the Nettlebed Estate in the South Oxfordshire Chilterns to make sure that no pheasants had been left behind, dead or wounded, after a shoot the day before. He and a friend between them had six dogs, mostly black Labradors.

After working through a larch wood, they went on along a muddy lane flanked by hedges until they came to a small T-junction. There they stopped for a minute as their pack hunted out some brambles round an old chalk pit; but when they moved on, they found they had only five dogs instead of six.

A check revealed that the missing one was Brooke, a six-year-old pedigree Labrador bitch – an excellent, experienced dog, worth at least £1,000. At first Neville thought she must have gone off on the line of a running pheasant, although this seemed unlikely, as one of the men would surely have seen her go. She had vanished so suddenly that 'it seemed as if a hand had come down out of the clouds and snatched her up'.

They called, whistled and searched in every possible direction, hampered by the strong, blustering wind, which made it difficult to hear. Soon suspicion centred round an old well, full of water and surrounded by barbed wire, a yard or two out in the field on the south side of the lane. Even though there were no scratch-marks on its concrete lip, and probing with sticks turned up no body, Neville had an inexplicable feeling that the bitch was somewhere very close, and this notion kept pulling him back to the spot.

At 1.30 he drove home – some thirteen miles – for a quick lunch. Then he came back with his wife Janet and the same friend, and the three of them searched till after dark. All independently felt the same instinct to return to the original site, and at one stage they thought they heard barking – only for the noise to be whipped away by the wind. After going home for tea, they returned yet again and stayed out till 10.30 pm.

On Monday morning they began once more and stayed out all day. The weather was still extremely wild and sound did not carry; but, although still haunted by the feeling that Brooke was not far away, Neville widened his search, thinking she might have got hung up in a fence, or been run over or even picked up by somebody on the main road. Again he went home without success.

Then, at eight on Tuesday morning, just as it was getting light, Cecil Chilcott, head keeper on the estate, walked down the valley after feeding his pheasants in a wood to the west. At last the wind had died and the morning was still. Suddenly, in the silence, he heard faint barking. There was something weird about the sound, for although it was reaching him quite audibly, he could not locate its origin, and as he moved in attempts to pin it down, it seemed to shift as well.

Experimental manoeuvring led him up on to a low bank, right beside the lane, and he realized that the noise was coming from underground, almost beneath his feet. There, under some elder bushes, he found a hole about eighteen inches across – the opening of an old well or water-tank.

He could not see the bottom of it, but when he called down, the bitch whined back at him; so, having comforted her, he hurried home to ring her owner and tell him that at least the animal was alive. Neville telephoned the local fire brigade for help and set off at once; the gamekeeper, meanwhile, returned to the well with a torch and stayed with the captive until help arrived.

Without waiting for the professionals, they tied a rope round Neville's waist and lowered him into the hole. To his immense relief, Brooke seemed none the worse. Her prison turned out to be a circular chamber about seven feet in diameter with cement-rendered walls, and on the soft mud underfoot lay the bones of some sizeable animal.

Earth and debris, falling in over the years, had built up a conical mound in the centre; and, by standing on this, Neville was just able to hand the Labrador up to his brother, who reached down through the opening. But when the others tried to pull him out, they found it was impossible, for he kept coming to rest under the lip of the hole and could not get up through it. Panic threatened; but, when the firemen arrived, they put up a tripod over the opening, lowered a harness and winched him up, so that he emerged, in the gamekeeper's words, 'like a cork out of a bottle'.

The way Brooke reacted to her release would surely have earned the praise of Mrs Thatcher: after a quick drink from a nearby puddle, she went straight back to the job of hunting for pheasants as if she had been delayed by nothing worse than a tiresome interruption. Even so, Neville felt certain that she must have been knocked out by the impact of her fall. Otherwise he would surely have heard her barking in the first few minutes after she had vanished, for he had spent some time standing within five or six yards of the subterranean cavity. Another strange fact is that the other dogs did not tell to where she was.

The rescue inevitably raised speculation about why the two wells were built there, less than fifty yards apart. They could have been meant for drainage, to take the storm water from the lane. What seems more likely, however, is that they formed a watering point for horses, for the lane was once the highway from Henley-on-Thames to Oxford and is still known locally as the Old Oxford Road.

Two aspects of the incident fascinate me. One is the way in which nature gradually obliterates man's artefacts. Examination showed that the dry well had in the distant past been covered over with wire-netting and earth, in which bracken and nettles had taken root; but its entrance had been hidden for so long that nobody who lived on the estate – not even people who had been there for more than forty years – had the slightest inkling of its existence.

Even stranger was the way in which the searching humans felt the bitch's close proximity. They could not analyse or explain how the communication came, but it reached them clearly enough. It heartens me to think that we all have a sixth sense, which might one day come to our own rescue.

Split over the old oak tree

As winter goes on, I become increasingly preoccupied with firewood. Is my supply going to hold out? There are few better sights than that of a shed stocked with a balanced mixture: clean, hard, white, easily split ash; tough, long-lasting beech and oak; cherry, quick-burning but inclined to spit; birch to lend a Nordic tang to the smoke; elm that smells a touch sour, but gives tremendous heat in the right stove . . .

There must be something atavistic in the pleasure of handling wood; and there is certainly a deep-seated feeling among country people that they have a right to collect firewood from the land round about. Often this privilege is none too well defined, with the result that on many estates competition rages between the forester, who is officially in charge but has not time to police the ground system-atically, and freelance woodcutters who pounce on anything that dies or is blown over.

I have to admit that in my day I have swagged away a good few trees; and on one memorable occasion, when we lived in the Chilterns, a forester was heard to cry out in exasperation: 'There isn't a bloody dead tree on this bloody estate, but what bloody Duff Hart-Davis is stood under it with his bloody power-saw, waiting for the bloody thing to fall down!'

It was not a question of 'or words to that effect'. Those were the words – and more broke out later over what became locally famous as the blasted oak. This large tree was riven by lightning during a summer storm, split clean down the middle as if by a celestial axe. One half fell to the ground, and the other, though shattered and useless as timber, remained upright.

For eighteen months we waited for the forester to clear the wreck away; he did nothing, and in the end temptation overcame us. My son and I set to, but because the tree was so big we took several afternoons to cut it up and cart it off.

Inevitably, the forester got wind of what was happening and on day three he strode up to one of the gamekeepers: 'Who's cutting up the blasted oak then?' he demanded; and Bill, though he knew perfectly well, answered quick as a flash: 'Someone with a blasted power saw, I should imagine.' Whereupon, in Bill's immortal phrase, the forester 'kicked his hat half way from here to High Wycombe'.

Now, it is a frustrating experience for amateur woodcutters who live in the west to travel eastwards and observe the unprecedented harvest scattered by the hurricane of October 1987. Grateful as I am to have escaped the wrath of that mighty wind, I cannot repress pangs of cupidity when I see tons of firewood still lying in the path of the storm.

It is not so much the stricken giants of the forest, which will yield good timber, that arouse my wood-lust. Rather it is the tangle of fallen branches and trunks of manageable proportions that call for immediate action. My inclination is to hitch a trailer to the jeep and set off for Kent or Sussex: have chainsaw, will travel.

For the past dozen years we hewers of firewood have been living in the fools' paradise created by Dutch elm disease. Instead of having to scrounge for fallen trunks or broken-off boughs, we suddenly found ourselves surrounded by hundreds of trees that had died, so to speak, with their boots on, and stood there gently drying out. Some fell, and began to rot with the wet; but these could be tackled first, and those still upright could be left, in natural cold-storage, until they were needed.

Mature elm is the devil to split – and some big trunks have such a twisted grain that the only practical way of reducing them to lumps of usable size is to saw them into cubes, cutting not only across the grain, but down it as well, a laborious business. Smaller trees – wych elms particularly – split easily and, although they tend to smell sour, they are unbeatable for wood-burning stoves.

Now, alas, the elms have almost gone, and the few that remain have been dead for so long that their wood is turning light and papery. Thus anyone wrongly placed to reap the benefit of the whirlwind is back to the former state of hunting for odds and ends, and of laying down green wood now, like wine, for use in two or three years' time. One of my last actions in 1987 was to split and stack a consignment of ash for use in 1989.

Most of my own wooding takes place on an extremely steep hill with a slope varying between one-in-four and one-in-two. The hazards of wielding a power-saw are in no way diminished by the fact that one is operating at an acute angle to the universe; but the worst problem is that of extracting the spoils. Gravity dictates that they must go down, to the tractor and trailer on the path below. The key question – on which visitors offer much gratuitous advice – is this: is it less effort to cut a tree into logs on its original site and roll the rounds down individually, or is it better to saw the tree into lengths and drag each one down to the path before logging it up there?

Either method has its drawbacks. If you try rolling short logs from a height, most of them lodge against other tree trunks or in the entrances to badger sets, so that you then have to scramble through half the wood to get them moving again. Some, on the other hand, take off as if propelled by demons and hurtle straight past the rendezvous: the other day an immense, ugly lump, weighing 150 lbs, crossed a footpath head-high at about forty knots and vanished into a field, luckily mine.

But dragging down six- or eight-foot lengths with a short rope is no picnic either. Often they too take off: suddenly you find yourself being given the bum's rush and, to avoid the twin perils of being knocked down or impacted face-first on a standing tree trunk, you are driven to footwork such as even Nijinsky would have hesitated to attempt.

Not the least advantage of such operations is that they are extremely strenuous. After a couple of hours of sawing, dragging, climbing, splitting and jumping for your life, you do not need an artificial workout in the gym or a session in the sauna. Your requirements, in fact, are extremely simple, amounting to no more than a very hot bath and a very large whisky, sipped before a roaring wood fire.

Mercy mission comes unstuck

When one receives a *cri de coeur* for help, it is only civil to answer the call; but I must admit that if the scene of the trouble is on someone else's ground, fresh to you, an element of adventure enters the reckoning and makes any expedition more attractive. Thus, when a farmer some four miles off rang up to say that his winter corn was being murdered by rabbits, I and two gamekeepers set out to the rescue full of enthusiasm and seasonal goodwill.

The field under siege was bordered by a long sweep of beech wood, and it was from there that the rabbits had been emerging at night. We therefore planned to work the dogs through the brambles along the inside of the wood, where we expected the rabbits to be lying.

Clearance had already been obtained for us to try the first stretch of woodland. The only potentially difficult area was at the bottom corner of the field, where two high-class houses were tucked into the trees. We planned, if possible, to get permission from the owners as we reached them.

At first all went well. On our pass down the wood we got four rabbits. At the edge of the first house's garden we met the owner, who was delighted for us to carry on. We added another couple to the bag.

At the second house, however, I called a temporary halt, for the chatelaine was said to be highly strung, and we did not want to upset her. Having told Bill and Cecil to hang on, I presented myself for a parley.

It took some time for my ring on the bell to be answered. Then the door opened a few inches. It was Herself, beyond doubt: a lady of substantial build, calling to mind a Wagnerian soprano, with a rather small, round face, *very* small pointed feet, and several acres of pink housecoat separating one from the other.

She seemed extraordinarily nervous, hovering on tiptoe, with her hands pointed downwards and outwards, like those of an Edward Lear character, and fluttering slightly, as though at any moment she might levitate through sheer alarm. I realized that in my Kammo smock, with a gun under one arm, I did not cut the most reassuring of figures; but I sought by fast talking to establish some sort of an understanding; rabbits eating the corn, called in by Mr X, hope she didn't mind . . .

I think I was making progress. At any rate she had managed to utter a couple of syllables indicating that she would not object if we dogged out her few acres . . . when all at once old Bill let drive with his magnum 12-bore in the shrubbery.

The report was stupendous. Magnified by the fancy brick carport, it buffeted me, rattled the house, and so shook the owner that she gave a single, bloodcurdling contralto shriek and flew straight up the staircase, disappearing feet last in an unforgettable vertical take-off.

I called some apologies after her, but got no answer, so I withdrew, closing the door quietly and went to remonstrate with my henchmen. 'Idiot!' I said. 'She went up like the Shuttle. You've probably given her a heart attack.'

'Bugger!' cried Bill indignantly. 'Bloody rabbit ran right across the lawn.'

I saw that restraint had been impossible. But somehow that one ill-timed detonation seemed to change our luck, for we got nothing else in the afternoon, and our errand of mercy prematurely ran out of steam.

Swan song for Lancelot

Alas for Lancelot! For the first time in twenty-four winters the Grand Old Bewick Swan of Slimbridge has failed to come home. There is still a faint chance that he may arrive and if anyone spots a swan with the number 567 in black on a white ring on his left leg, that will be him; but since Elaine, his mate of the last ten years, arrived at Christmas without him, it looks very much as though he has met his end.

There is something heroic, not to say Arthurian, about the length of his career and the fidelity with which he returned every winter to Sir Peter Scott's wildfowl reserve at Slimbridge on the shore of the

Severn. When he first arrived, in 1962, he was already adult, and two or more years old. Thus, if he is still alive, he must be at least twenty-six.

One other Bewick swan is known to have reached the age of thirty, but he was a sedentary fellow who never did much travelling. Lancelot, by contrast, has always been a tireless commuter: on his annual migrations to and from the swans' breeding grounds in Novaya Zemblya, 2,500 miles to the north-east, he is calculated to have flown 130,000 miles, overflying the Iron Curtain twice a year.

One piece of good news is that the swans seem to have escaped unscathed from the effects of Chernobyl radiation. Earlier, staff at Slimbridge were afraid that their summer grazing might have been contaminated, but now it seems that breeding was good, and a healthy crop of cygnets has come in among the 300-strong flock that has settled for the winter.

Lancelot, never very prolific, sired relatively few offspring; so it is heartening to know that his daughter Pendragon and grandchild Percival (last year's cygnet) are now at Slimbridge. But the fact that Elaine has joined up with them in a family group reinforces the likelihood that the patriarch is gone.

🌿

Time for horse highways

I am not sure that many people have yet realized what a huge opportunity for change is presented by the Government's draft proposals for the future of the countryside. Even that vociferous lobby the National Farmers' Union now concedes that our land is producing too much food and that some acres must be taken out of agricultural production. The great question is: what should be done with those that do come out?

The planting of more woods and the replacement of some of the hedges which were mindlessly ripped out a generation ago will contribute much towards restoring the attractive appearance of devastated areas such as East Anglia. Yet I should like to see an innovation of more practical use to people who enjoy riding.

This would be the creation of a whole network – a green grid – of bridleways on which it would be possible to travel right across the country. Parts of the network already exist, I know, but it is relatively rare for bridleways to run through open farmland.

To create new ones, all farmers would have to do would be to stop ploughing up some of their headlands – that is, the strips next to hedge or fence where the tractor turns at the end of each furrow. At the moment most farmers plough to within inches of the edge of the field, but, if they were to leave a grass verge three or four yards wide uncultivated, it would cut down corn production (as is needed) and at the same time furnish a highway for horses.

Gates or jumping places would also be needed, and these would cost some money. But is not this the moment for farmers, who have received many millions of pounds of taxpayers' money in subsidies, to pay back a little of it in providing some basic facilities for recreation?

Travels with a trapeze

It is, I hope, a harmless eccentricity to own and use a trapeze. Of course the sight of a bar hanging in mid-air does sometimes provoke friends to let off ape-noises and even to shamble about the lawn with their knuckles on the ground; but the advantages of having the contraption always available far outweigh such occasional irritations.

To my trapeze I attribute the fact that – touch wood – I have never had any back problems. It may not make sense in medical terms, but a few upward circles every day seem to do wonders for the spine, and I know for a fact that, if I just dangle vertically by the hands for a minute or so, my backbone elongates from this form of natural traction so that my feet, having started off a couple of inches clear of the ground, gradually descend until they are almost brushing it. I also find it beneficial to hang upside down, like a bat: a process which not only gives a new look to the surroundings, but powerfully clears the brain.

A trapeze also provides a good deal of amusement, though this cannot be guaranteed to be harmless. Once a rather porky young man, who at the time was pursuing a sister-in-law and came to lunch in a natty tweed suit, could not resist a post-prandial rush at the apparatus hanging from the walnut tree. He went up well, but as his hands closed on the bar, a fearful rending sound burst from his midriff and with a cry he dropped to the ground like a poached egg. For a bad moment I thought he had ruptured himself, but it turned out only that his braces had dragged their moorings.

I like my trapezes to be home-made: a good, straight hazel stem nearly two inches thick and planed down to give a smooth grip makes an ideal bar. If it is slung on nylon cords with a breaking strain of about 1,500 lbs a side, it is not likely to collapse. Yet, as I know to my own cost, the wood does in the end deteriorate and go brittle; and sometimes I am haunted by thoughts of the trapezes I have left behind in the gardens of earlier homes. I can think of three that may by now have dumped some unwary successor suddenly on the ground, or may be about to do so. The moral seems to be that, when you shift camp, you should cut down your trapeze and take it with you.

Bone from the neck upwards

I wish I could see more clearly into the mind of Agamemnon, our Wiltshire Horn ram. Though down in the books by the name of the King of Mycenae, he is tending, in his increasingly thuggish behaviour, to resemble more and more the character whose name was suggested for him by my visiting sister-in-law: Rambo.

It may be that the heroic circumstances of his birth – during a blizzard, in the middle of last year's Grand National – have something to do with it. Certainly by the time he was four months old, and we took him to a local agricultural show, he had become extremely precocious.

He looked very handsome in a head-collar made from red mountaineering rope; but, being beginners, we had only the faintest hopes of success and were amazed when, in the class for unusual breeds, he carried off one prize after another – first a rosette and £8 in cash, then another rosette, then a large cup.

Back at home a neighbouring farmer said he had heard that the young ram had 'got a bit fruity' during the show. Against this charge I defended him stoutly. It was true that he had jumped about when the judge (a vet) repeatedly seized him by parts of his anatomy which other humans do not normally reach; but apart from this he had behaved with great aplomb. 'You watch him,' the farmer repeated, 'or one day he'll bloody 'ave yer.'

'No, no,' I said. 'He's quiet as a lamb.' But, as the months went by, I began to change my mind. At first the very close attention which he paid to humans seemed born of friendliness and curiosity; having been trained since infancy to come to a bucket, he would walk straight up to you and stand to have his chest scratched.

Gradually, however, his behaviour grew ambivalent. Sometimes, under the pretext of enjoying a scratch or holding a conversation, he would suddenly square up and threaten his interlocutor with a butt. The difficulty was – and is – to divine his mood, for no matter what he is thinking, his expression remains (if he will forgive me) sheepish, and only a lowering of the head or a quick lifting of the front feet betrays incipient aggression.

One afternoon before Christmas, as I knelt on the ground at the end of the cowshed, doing repairs to the stonework, he came up and stood with his forehead touching my cheek. For at least five minutes he remained in the closest possible proximity, breathing in my right ear, and as I worked, I reminded him of various matters – not least the fact that, if he became too obstreperous, he might easily end up in the deep-freeze. All the time I was poised to give him one with the handle of my cement trowel, should he turn rough, but he merely stood there till I had finished.

Then, a couple of days later, as I was planting an apple tree in the orchard, he wilfully misconstrued the movements of my spade for aggressive posturing and put in several undisguised charges. Since he must weigh at least 100 lbs and has a formidable pair of horns, such advances are not amusing. The best way to deal with them, if you are in a tight corner, is to take a good grip of him, one hand on a horn, the other in the fleece of his rump, and steer him off like a wheelbarrow.

Now, out in the field with his wives, he is distinctly aggressive and territorial. My neighbour was absolutely right: he will, if he can, 'bloody 'ave yer' – and as always in this kind of encounter, the worst thing anybody can do is to run away. Provided you stand your ground and face him, he keeps his distance; but the moment you turn your back, he launches himself in a springing arc.

How we can cure this habit, I am not at all sure. But the one certain fact is that there can be no point in trying to reason with him, for I fear that he is, in every sense of the phrase, bone from the neck upwards.

After the snow

For the first few days of the cold spell we had no real problems. We had bitter frost, it is true – down to −15°c – but only a dusting of snow, and it was easy enough to get out and about. From the western half of the country we watched the sufferings of the east, thankful that for once we had the better of the weather.

Then, on Tuesday night, the snow reached us. By morning it was shoulder-deep in our lane and only our neighbour's biggest tractor could get through to us. As usual in and after a blizzard the real cause of trouble was the wind, which filled every hollow as fast as it was cleared, blasted snow into the stables, soaking the horses' beds, and even, by means of an ingenious backlash, piled a thick crust on top of the logs in the woodshed.

Out in the fields and woods the effect was fascinating, for the smooth, clean blanket laid bare the events of the night for all to see. Here a badger had scrambled under the fence, here a hare had gone loping along the hill, here in this beaten patch flecked with fresh blood, a rabbit had been killed by a fox.

I have never had much doubt that our valley is alive with foxes and now I *know* it is – for there in the snow were innumerable fox tracks. During the night foxes had come and gone in every conceivable direction, down the footpath from the wood, across our fields, into our farmyard, through it, out the other side. One animal, I know, covers a lot of ground in a single night's hunting, but here was evidence that a whole army had been on the move, most of them heading, it seemed, for my beleaguered poultry.

Not the least tiresome feature of the freeze-up is that one spends so much time merely sorting things out every morning. First, hot water has to be carried laboriously out from the house to melt the ice in the animals' troughs and buckets. Then it is a question of the vehicles, one or more of which usually will not start.

The cold has been altogether too much for my old red tractor. Trying to jump-start it one morning, I rolled it out into the lane and headed downhill. The tractor, having declined to play ball, came to rest on the glacier at the bottom, half-blocking the narrow road.

Out with the jeep then; best to tow the machine back to base. Easier said than done: even in four-wheel drive, tyres spin on ice. Tractor remains *in situ*. Return to base for tools. Back to tractor. Take off battery. Bring battery back to farm. Connect to charger.

Spend time bringing in logs, etc. Then run battery back to tractor, fit it, creep up on starter-key to take it by surprise – and off she goes! But by now it is nearly lunchtime and nothing useful has been accomplished.

For some members of the household, though, the cold snap is not total disaster. At 7.50 one morning, with the outside temperature 14° below zero, our electricity went off, on, off. Down the drain went my early stint on the word-processor, the few paragraphs I had cobbled together vanished for ever. I sat back cursing.

But the two dogs, galvanized by the click of the computer switching off (which they know signifies the end of a session), sprang joyfully from their armchairs by the fire and rushed over saying, 'Breakfast! Breakfast!' And because I could not see to go on working, they got it ten minutes early.

Plumbing tip, rustic-style

During the week I have learned at least one useful plumbing tip. If your pipes freeze and are then thawed out, you will probably be left with an airlock in the hot water system. But there is one very simple way of shifting this, providing you have a hot and cold mixer unit on either bath or sink. All you do is block the outflow with your hand or a cloth, turn on the cold, and then turn on the hot, so that the cold water is forced up the hot pipe. Provided the system is not too complicated, it works like magic.

Case of the shrinking deer

Pictures of red deer coming down out of the snowbound Scottish Highlands in search of food give a grim reminder that *cervus elaphus* is essentially a woodland animal now condemned by the disappearance of the ancient Caledonian forest to live on bare, unsheltered hills.

Over the centuries the Highland deer have performed an extraordinary feat of adaptation, reducing themselves to half the size of their ancestors in attempts to combat the harshness of their environment.

There is a striking difference between animals which subsist on the treeless uplands and their genetically ideal brethren lucky enough to enjoy the warmth and shelter of a forest. A hill stag weighing 220 lbs is reckoned a good one, but a woodland stag of 400 lb is nothing exceptional.

In the open, even a normal winter takes a severe toll. The Red Deer Commission, which monitors population and culling from its headquarters in Inverness, positively expects some 2,000 stags, 4,000 hinds and up to 5,000 calves to die of hunger and cold between January and April. In other words, more than two per cent of the adult population will go under, and up to twelve per cent of the young. But, if the weather proves severe, mortality is much higher. (It is this that makes annual culling not merely humane, but a vital necessity, for without it suffering would be infinitely greater.)

In woodland, by contrast, there is almost no mortality at all – first because the deer have shelter, and second because, even in deep snow, they can usually find food. Bramble leaves are a favourite, and even yew, although poisonous if eaten to excess, goes down well in small quantities. Species of deer such as fallow and roe that inhabit our southern woods are usually as fat as butter, no matter how cold it becomes.

The last really severe winter in the Highlands was that of 1962–3. Mortality was savage, and up to seventy per cent of the previous summer's calves were lost. Since then, however, a series of relatively mild winters has allowed the red deer population to build up to its present, highest-ever figure of nearly 300,000.

Some people may find it odd that the deer have done so well in spite of everything – in spite of their environment, in spite of poaching, and in spite of the fact that they are energetically culled every year: the hinds by Highland professionals, the stags by amateur stalkers paying large amounts of money for the privilege of getting soaked, frozen, baked and exhausted in stunningly beautiful surroundings.

But the fact is – no matter how distasteful it may be to the anti-field-sports lobby – that nothing better ensures the future of any creature, be it deer, tiger, rhino, fox or pheasant, than to be preserved as a sporting quarry.

Seventy-year-old ammunition

To defend their preserves against nocturnal marauders countless gamekeepers use alarm guns, which usually consist of a thin wire or cord stretched between trees at chest height across a path and a simple mechanism that fires a blank cartridge if anyone or anything puts pressure on the wire. Of course the devices can be triggered by deer or falling branches; and if, in the morning, a keeper finds that one of them has gone off, he cannot usually tell what sprang it. Nevertheless, the guns make useful deterrents, for it takes a poacher with strong nerves to stand his ground if he has just punctured the night with a deafening report and does not know who else may have heard it.

It was thus with some annoyance that a friend of mine found he was getting misfires: several times, although something had run into a wire during the night, the cartridge had not detonated. When he cut one of the blanks open he was amazed to find, on the inside of the waxed-cardboard closure-wad, the legend 'Eley New Load No. 6' and the date '1914'. Another read '1916'.

The cartridge cases are made of red plastic and are, therefore, obviously modern, but is it really possible that the end-wads were made during or before the First World War?

A call to the Eley factory in Birmingham. Chris Carver, the marketing director: 'Nothing to do with us. The blanks are manufactured for us by the Caledonian Cartridge Company.' A call to the CCC in Angus. 'Nothing to do with us. All we do is make up materials we get from Eley.' Back to Birmingham. Questioned further, Carver admits that there *could* have been some old cardboard originally stamped for game cartridges which was used for the blanks, but that it must have all gone now.

Maybe it has. But is it not rather amazing that there are still, in nightly use, components of ammunition which were already in existence at the time of or before the Battle of the Somme?

It's all in the soil

Twelve days after the thaw set in, beautifully sculpted snowdrifts still line the walls along the edges of fields on top of the hill – a reminder of how much colder it is up there than where our house stands, two-thirds of the way down. Already, however, the sheer destructive power of the recent weather is becoming apparent. You might not think that the elements could reduce rock to powder – but they can. Here, in exposed places, rain driven by wind forced its way horizontally into the walls and then, as it froze, burst stones asunder, reducing whole stretches to rubble.

Now, as I get going again on my vegetable garden, the frailty of human existence is borne in on me by the thought that the rich loam which I am turning over is essentially limestone: soaked, frozen, exploded, ground down and washed off the hill over thousands of years.

What sort of creatures lived here when what I am digging was rock? Did they too grow food or did they merely hunt? The second, I guess. In any case, it is I who now benefit from erosion, for I can dig down two spade-depths unimpeded by rock or clay.

Other beneficiaries include moles, which have been excavating like maniacs ever since the ground softened. Provided they do not tunnel actually under the lawn, I do not mind them sharing my ground – and in fact they do me a service by throwing up heaps of the finest tilth imaginable, which I collect and dump on the garden.

Sometimes it strikes me that most of one's life consists of moving (in cosmic terms) minute amounts of matter from one place to another, be they cart-loads of manure, barrowfuls of earth, bucketfuls of wood-ash or merely specks of household dust.

Finding job satisfaction

It looks a bit as though I had hired a gorilla for a workmate, but in fact I am proud to claim the work as my own: a small piece of genuine stone-walling. Winston Churchill, we know, used to find relaxation in building brick walls at Chartwell, and I can see why; but I reckon stonework is even more satisfying, since it is that much more massive.

Mine is what is known in these parts as a 'muck' wall – that is, not dry stone, but built with muck or mortar. All I did was fill in the bottom half of an obsolete doorway in the side of a barn, but in the course of this modest accomplishment I learned a good deal. Not least, I discovered what a phenomenal weight of material goes into a small area. I calculate that the ingredients of *my* wall, which is not much more than a metre square, must have weighed well over a ton. I also found out that you need to have confidence in your materials. At first the muck I was using seemed to have no adhesive properties and kept falling out of the joints; then I began to see that – as in other activities – if enough muck is slung, some of it does stick. I also discovered that a shot of washing-up liquid in the water makes the muck easier to handle.

Now, with the benefit of this experience and some instruction from friendly local professionals, I can talk with discernment about how rotten sand is these days (either too sharp or too muddy) and the relative merits of cut-pointing or bag-finish. I cannot say that my own work exhibits either of these to a marked degree – yet, armed with my new-found skill, I feel that, as a mason, I am ready to reach for the sky.

FEBRUARY

As lanes go, ours is a pretty good one. Arched over with hazel, elder and sycamore, it plunges down a precipitous hill between banks which in summer are carpeted with wild flowers. You might think that passers-by would hesitate before fouling so attractive a place with litter. Not at all: every few weeks I feel obliged to hold a purge and collect up every scrap of paper, every burger box, every beer can, crisp packet, wine bottle and plastic bag; but then, in a few days, more mess starts to appear.

Most of it, I feel sure, is not the work of walkers or other local people, who on the whole are tidy and do not jettison more than the odd sweet-paper. The majority of it is imported, being thrown out of passing cars.

If the Government really means to succeed in its drive to clean up Britain, it needs also to commission serious research into the psychology of drivers: to find out why, once they are behind the wheel, they behave so atrociously – not merely in the business of motoring, but in their general contempt for everything outside their own little capsule.

The secret, I believe, lies in the simple fact that the occupants of cars are on the move, for ever going somewhere else. Though they may *think* they are in the country, they in fact have no contact with the environment, but merely pass through it in a tin can, unable to hear, smell or feel anything going on around them. They have no commitment to or compassion for the landscape and, as they whiz past, they do not realize that every field and wood belongs to some individual, just as much as their own gardens belong to them. Besides, the chances of their revisiting any particular spot are remote – and all these factors combine to produce an attitude of mind which sees no wrong in hurling the by-products of picnics and snacks out of the windows.

In our immediate area the most vulnerable place of all is a little earth track that leads off the lane and into the wood on the brow of the hill. Because it is secluded, it is the favourite resort of what are decorously known as 'courting couples', who drive into it at night and get down to business. If that were all they did, it would not be too bad. But during their sessions they throw out rubbish of every description, including objects too sordid to mention – and here, too, periodic clear-ups merely leave the ground free for fresh infestation, as the site is also used for general rubbish-dumping.

The ultimate insult came the other evening, when I found two double-bed mattresses thrown down the steep bank beside the track. (I do not mean that these had been brought there for courting purposes, merely thrown away.) Enraged, and intending to return in the morning with a trailer so that I could take them to the nearby tip, I pulled them up on to the path. This, however, was not good enough for the next visitor, who flung them down the bank again and left in their place unmistakable evidence of what he had been up to during the night.

Counter-measures are needed, and the most effective one will be to bar the neck of the path with a trench, easily crossed by walkers, riders and tractors on legitimate business, but deep enough to stop the sleazy suburban vehicles of midnight cowboys.

Overrun by foxes

Suddenly the place is alive with foxes. We are never by any means short of them, but during the past few weeks there seems to have been a population explosion. Reason dictates that this is not possible – for cubs are born only in the early spring – and that what we are witnessing is a population shift.

If the causes of this are obscure, its effect is spectacular. The other afternoon, to our chagrin, we saw four foxes sitting out in our top field all at once. They seemed to be taking the air or measuring the distance to our hen house, but in fact I think they were resting after nocturnal labours, for the rut is in full swing and this quartet looked like gentlemen knackered by the strain of following a lady on heat.

At night the valleys echo with the dry, staccato 'roff, roff, roff' of the dogs and the yowling of the vixens. So preoccupied are they all with procreation that they lose some of their normal caution – and this leads to exciting encounters.

One morning this week, as I walked along the edge of a wood at first light, modestly trying out a few bars from *Il Trovatore*, I glimpsed movement over the skyline to my left. Rising on tip-toe, I saw a big dog fox coming in across the winter wheat.

My two Labradors were trotting up the edge of the wood ahead of me, on a course converging with that of the fox. I quickly realized that because of a hump in the field they would not be able to see it, or it them, until they were close together. I therefore stood still and waited.

On came the fox, sniffing about. On went the dogs. At last one of them looked up – and did a tremendous double-take. A second later all three animals were travelling at maximum velocity, the fox leading by the length of a cricket pitch. Because the dogs had the inside track, he could not immediately gain the safety of the wood, but was given a scorching run for 300 yards before he was able to dive through a hedge and go to ground.

No such escape saved another fox, which I found a day later lying freshly dead in the middle of a field. The cause of its death was obvious – it had been shot through the chest by a .22 rifle bullet – but we could not make out who had killed it. The farmer had heard a shot at eight that morning and had gone out to investigate, but had seen nobody about. There is no gamekeeper on that stretch of land. And what poacher – if it was one – would bother to shoot a fox or, if he did, leave its body lying in the open?

Thoughts on skinning and splitting

It is not every day that the editor of a national newspaper telephones to ask how he should deal with a muntjac which he has just shot. But when one does, I of course give him the best advice I can.

In case anybody is in doubt, the muntjac or barking deer is native to India and Japan, and the ancestors of those now resident in England were imported by the eleventh Duke of Bedford, who established a stock in his park at Woburn Abbey during the early years of this century. Their descendants find the western world much to their liking: they have fanned out widely from that first base and now inhabit large areas of woodland in the south of the country. To me they are the least attractive of our deer, being rather piglike in appearance with their heads carried lower than their rumps. But they make up for any aesthetic shortcomings by being extremely good to eat.

When my friend rang, I told him exactly what to do: hang the animal in a cold place for at least a week and then skin it, still in a vertical attitude, beginning at the hocks and working downwards. With such a small carcase – not much more than 20 lbs – butchery is a simple matter, and after that it is up to the cook.

Yet even as I gave my advice, I fell to wondering how many people would now be capable of doing the job. A hundred years ago a high proportion of the population would not have baulked at the idea of wringing a chicken's neck or even slaughtering a pig. Yet how many nowadays would tackle such messy tasks rather than go to the supermarket and buy frozen meat? (I do not mean in some crisis like the aftermath of a nuclear holocaust, but now in everyday life.) Partly, of course, it is a question of squeamishness, of sensibilities rendered altogether too fine by packaging, convenience foods and life in cities, far from the front line; but what worries me more than that is the disappearance of fundamental skills which our predecessors took for granted.

Sometimes, if an energetic visitor asks what he can do to make himself useful, I suggest that he goes and splits a few logs. But do I just turn him loose in the woodshed? Not at all, because the odds are that he will have no idea how to use an axe.

If left undirected, he grips the end of the handle with one fist and the middle of it with the other – and thus, with hands locked, he starts swinging ineffectively. He does not realize that in this attitude he has a good chance of rupturing himself, a better one of snapping the head of the axe right off by overreaching and none at all of splitting the wood cleanly. He has no conception of how tremendously the descent of the axe-head is accelerated, how spectacularly the power of its blow increased, if he will only keep his upper hand loose and let it slide the length of the handle each time he swings. He has lost – or never known – a skill first learned by man several thousand years ago.

I do not say that the ability to wield an axe or skin a muntjac is a prerequisite of survival in the 1980s, but I do in an old-fashioned way cling to the belief that the more things one can do competently for oneself, the richer one's life becomes and the less of a nuisance one is to other people.

Fairy ice in the morning

Moving through the woods early the other morning, I was puzzled to find elongated white shapes showing up all over the forest floor. In the half-dark they looked like trails of snow, but no snow had fallen for weeks; rather, the preceding days had been warm and atrociously wet, until a sudden frost had come in during the night. I began to think that the unprecedented rainfall must have led to an outbreak of mould and that what I was seeing was some sort of winter fungus.

As the light came up, I grew still more fascinated by the little white streaks: they were everywhere and the mould (or whatever it was) seemed to have grown at extraordinary speed, for it certainly had not been there the day before. Most of it was heaped on top of dead sticks about an inch in diameter lying horizontally just off the ground. Thicker branches or ones that had lodged vertically bore none.

Not until I bent down and touched one did I realize that the strange excrescences were made of ice – and no ordinary ice either, but the most beautifully delicate leaves and whorls of it, built up of innumerable strands finer than the silkiest hair. Some of them stood up two inches or more above the surface of the wood, as exquisitely sculpted as frost-flowers on a windowpane, but three-dimensional.

What I think had happened was that the sticks had been absolutely sodden and with the abrupt onset of frost the water lodged in the outer cells had suddenly frozen. These outer layers, expanding, had compressed the moisture trapped inside and this had then been forced out in minute jets or fountains, which themselves froze as they hit the air.

The effect was magical and mysterious – as if a master chef had piled each twig with spun sugar; but when I tried to break off a piece for a closer examination, I found that it could not be done, for at the slightest touch the fairy ice melted and simply vanished.

In favour of hibernation

Much as I hate most circulars, I positively look forward to those from the British Hedgehog Preservation Society, for the engaging qualities of the creature seem to come through strongly in propaganda issued on its behalf. Thus the latest 'Know Your Hedgehog' leaflet tells you how to build escape ramps so that the animals can extricate themselves from cattle grids or other potential death traps. The ramp, says the leaflet reassuringly, need not be elaborate. 'It is but a slope of about twenty degrees in one corner of the pit', preferably made of concrete, with the surface left rough 'to enable the escapee to gain foothold'.

Another new fact sheet, on hibernation, describes how in autumn hedgehogs build nests called 'hibernacula' of dried leaves and other vegetation in piles of brushwood, compost heaps or rabbit burrows. There they settle down for the winter, bodies cooling, heart-rate falling, and respiration slowing so much that they breathe only once every six minutes.

Their immobility, of course, makes them vulnerable to predators such as foxes, but, although most of them wake up fairly often during the winter, they rarely leave their nests. Their intermittent 'arousals' may be caused by disturbance or unexpectedly warm weather.

In many ways their mode of life seems enviable, and the idea of going into a trancelike sleep for the winter is thoroughly agreeable. The chances are that if you were suddenly got by a fox, you would

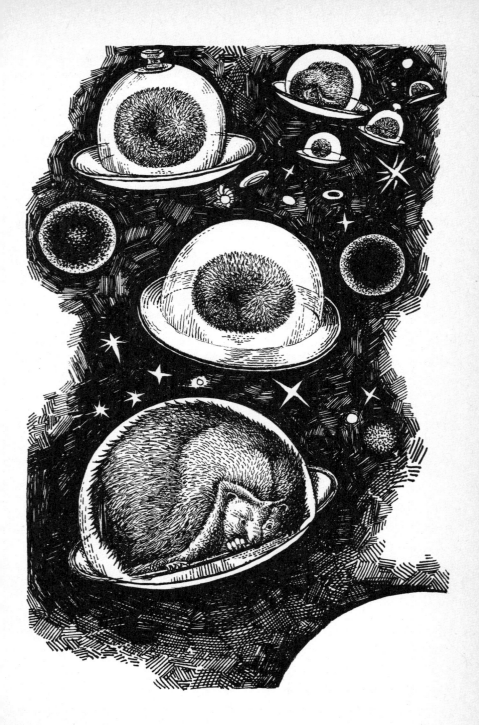

not know much about it; and as long as you avoided that fate, you would awake – after perhaps the odd arousal for a nip of whisky – to find it was spring.

Sure enough the leaflet points out that the mechanisms of hibernation might with advantage be applied to humans. Astronauts and other explorers could make long-duration expeditions without having to carry large quantities of food; and, since during the winter shutdown physical damage is less traumatic to an animal's body, 'there is medical interest in hibernation as a way of improving the tolerance of human bodies to major surgical operations'.

Outlandish dawn chorus

Anyone passing our gate these days may well wonder what on earth is going on in the farmyard, for the matutinal noises are hardly what you would call relaxing.

With any luck dawn is greeted by nothing worse than a crow-in or screech-up from the cockerels, but at or after first light there often breaks out the fearful yowling that signifies a good cat fight, as Pussy, our neighbour's tom, seeks to assert his territorial rights over our own Kitty, who arrived only at Christmas.

A couple of powerful human roars put paid to this particular cacophony, even if they increase the overall decibel level. But even as Pussy scoots for home, one of the sheep has decided that it is breakfast time and bleats for rations with a noise indistinguishable from that of a child which, as it is violently sick, makes no effort to control itself. Simultaneously, the Labrador bitch in season launches into her repertoire of two-tone, Baskerville-type howls – and it is when Shalimar the peacock lets drive in the middle of this ululation with a volley of brazen, jungle-splitting screams that I see early passers-by accelerate on their way with looks of incredulity and apprehension.

News hounds in action

Alert readers have pointed out that, if I take my dogs out for two walks a day, I will make about 700 excursions in the course of the year, rather than 350 as I claimed recently. True enough; and if one *is* going to spend that amount of time and energy on canine recreation, one might as well try to assess the benefits that accrue to either party.

For myself, fresh air and exercise are the immediate advantages; and besides them there is the fact that walking often seems to free the mind, helping to solve old problems and produce new ideas. But I cannot believe that it is considerations of this kind which make the dogs leap in the air the moment I look like getting on the move.

Of course, if I pick up a gun, we enter another world, since Labradors are bred for shooting and in their view the pursuit of game takes precedence over every other activity. Yet the prospect of a routine walk excites them nearly as much.

Obviously they too enjoy the exercise, but I hardly think they run because they know it is good for them. Nor do they care a fig for fiery dawns, glowing sunsets or stirring views – things that help lift humans above the drudgery of putting one foot in front of the other. (They do, however, respond to some features of the landscape. For instance, they like looking down steep hills and often, when we emerge from a wood on to a grass field, the expanse of sloping turf sets them off racing crazily in circles, each trying to wrong foot the other by ridiculously sudden changes of direction.) Yet their main enjoyment, I feel certain, derives from having a good look round, of seeing what they can find, of discovering what has gone on in the night. In this they are very like journalists – and if I were to describe them as news hounds, I do not think I would be far wrong.

Of course, they are always hoping to pick up the trail of a pheasant, rabbit or hare: a touch of any of these, even of a squirrel, will put them instantly into overdrive and may lead to a satisfactory chase, perhaps even to a capture. But their principal concern is to analyse the evidence of the environment and find out what changes have taken place recently.

In areas frequented by other dogs, much of the information concerns their own kind; but in more remote areas, such as we tend to head for, the only other users of the paths are wild creatures. Hence the minute care with which the dogs sniff individual stalks of grass and twigs bent over the path. Often the analysis of one scent takes a minute or more and evidently it can yield a wealth of information – not only that a fox or badger passed this way, but when and what it was doing.

Since almost every trace of scent demands a riposte in kind, there is frequent – not to say constant – squatting and lifting of legs; and over the years our elder bitch, Pansy, has perfected an elegant, elaborate technique known in the family (with due deference to French skiing terminology) as the widdle *artistique*.

For humans, the sad fact is that our senses are too blunt to be able to share this secret world. If I actually see a fox, find footprints, come on spots of blood in the snow or a tuft of fur caught on the barbed wire, I get a glimpse of it; but until someone invents a computer that can translate canine thought into human speech, most of it will remain closed to me and, as I trudge through the woods, I shall have to accept the fact that the dogs know far more about what has been going on than I do.

And what do they do with all the information? Subconsciously they salt it away into their own primaeval computers, where it gradually builds into the priceless commodity which humans call experience.

Storm force in Barra

I feel particular sympathy for Bernie, the bull who drowned while trying to swim from Barra to the smaller island of Vatersay, since I myself once had an unnerving experience in those wild Hebridean waters.

It occurred when the explorer John Ridgway was returning from his latest voyage round the globe in his yacht *English Rose VI*. When, at Christmas 1983, he sent a radio message from somewhere south of New Zealand telling me to meet him off Barra for the last leg of the trip to his home at Ardmore, on the north-west tip of Sutherland, I thought he was joking.

Not at all. As he came up the Bay of Biscay, all set to break the record for a non-stop circumnavigation, his messages became more insistent; and so it was that I paraded on the little quay of

Castlebay, at Barra's southern tip, before dawn on a raging February morning.

Many boatmen would have found an excuse for not putting out into that roaring darkness, but John Allan Maclean was unmoved by the force nine gale and away we went, heaving and plunging in the tubby little boat that normally acted as the inter-island ferry. Ridgway's last radio message, relayed through his home, had said he would pick me up at first light in the lee of Muldoanich Island, an outlier of Vatersay, so we headed south-eastwards into ever more mountainous seas.

At first we could see nothing at all, and we narrowly escaped extermination beneath the bows of the incoming Caledonian Macbrayne steamer, which loomed above us like the *Titanic*. But as dawn crept into the leaden sky we began to make out the black shapes of islands on our starboard beam. Then suddenly, way ahead of us, a single green light appeared for a few seconds. 'There he is!' cried Maclean. 'That's him.'

Sure enough, up came Ridgway on the boat's radio. 'For Christ's sake keep well away from me,' he ordered. 'I don't want to get smashed up now.' Ten minutes later, in a never-to-be-forgotten moment, we sighted the yacht herself, heeling steeply to show her white hull with the skipper and his mate clinging like crimson-suited crabs to the sky-blue deck.

When we closed with them, the wind was so strong that the rubber dinghy which Ridgway let out on the end of a line spun like a leaf in mid-air for several seconds before landing upside down on the water. As a result, I was none too dry by the time he dragged me aboard. But, unlike poor Bernie, I survived the crossing – and so did my supply of whisky and fresh milk, the first the mariners had tasted in 200 days and 28,000 miles.

A sojourn with Ridgway at his adventure school could hardly be described as relaxing. At seven every morning (six in the summer), wet or fine, he has you out there running over the mountains on a diabolical, up-and-down three-mile course. Only those quick-witted enough to invent debilitating injuries can escape this shattering start to the day; and later, if you do not climb a mountain or go sailing, there is bound to be a workout on the machines in his private gym. But for those who can stick it, the experience is richly rewarding, for Ridgway is one of the few people who has managed to make a living right out in the wilds, and it is here, on the rocky coast of Sutherland, that he comes into his own.

There is no road to his croft, which is perched high above a sea loch and looks across to the great hills whose names – among them Arkle and Foinaven – the Duchess of Westminster has bestowed upon her racehorses. To reach the place at all you have either to walk the last two miles, carrying your kit or, if the weather is calm enough, cross the loch in a small boat.

Ridgway supports himself by writing and by putting children and businessmen through the adventure school. That the courses have a profound effect on almost everyone who takes them is due in no small measure to the impact of his own personality. In urban settings he is apt to become chippy and aggressive, but here at home his natural ruggedness matches that of the landscape so well that visitors draw strength from him, just as they do from sudden, violent confrontation with the mountains and the sea.

I watched in amazement as he pitched into a new batch of young executives from a biscuit firm. Poor wretches, they staggered out of a bus at the end of a long journey looking sick as dogs and were immediately told to change – men standing on the beach, girls in an old shed – so that they had bathing gear next to the skin and were suitably clad for spending forty-eight hours in the open.

As they went down the sea loch in a fishing boat, Ridgway ordered them to give up any food they were hoarding. Sheepishly they produced Mars bars, apples and carefully saved sandwiches, all of which were dumped in a bucket. Then they learned that they were going to spend the night on an uninhabited island, without shelter, and that they would have nothing to eat but any raw fish they managed to catch.

Disbelief made them gape when Ridgway told them to strip off, stuff their clothes into a black polythene bin-liner, jump overboard and swim to the island. Yet when he shouted 'Jump!' over the side they went like lambs, plummeting into the icy water.

'What makes them all obey you?' I asked. 'Why don't some of them refuse?'

'I don't know,' he said with a grin. 'But they never do. They jump, every time.'

Counting the Highland deer

Launched by a council of war on the glen road, we start climbing away to the first horizon above us. Beyond that line of grass, heather and rock, the snow-covered tops gleam blinding white against the sky. The wind is keen from the north-west.

Once again the eight-man team of the Red Deer Commission is taking to the hills for its annual count. All are in tweed plus-fours and most (to my surprise) wear green Wellingtons rather than walking boots. My companion is Dick Youngson, a senior officer of the Commission, and we have been deployed in a huge oblong formation to take in part of Reay Forest, the mountain wilderness in Sutherland belonging to the Westminster family. We are at the south-eastern end of the oblong. Next on our right, out of sight in the neighbouring glen, is Alex Dempster, known as Acky. Every man has been carefully positioned and directed so that he can cover any ground out of his neighbour's sight.

The aim is to get all the deer on the move and count them as accurately as possible, breaking down each herd into males, females and calves. As Dick explains, the idea is *not* 'to roll a great mass of deer forward in front of us', but rather to spill them back through the cordon so that they can be accurately recorded. Much depends on communications – and these are excellent. Soon the air is crackling with messages passed from one walkie-talkie radio to another. Here is Acky, calling us from the north-east: 'There's a puckle stags right above you. Are you seeing them yet? Over.'

'Not yet, Ack. But they're all right. Either they'll move up when they spot us, or they'll get our wind and go forward.'

Now – there goes a mobile thicket of antlers, hurrying up the ridge above us, in the direction we want, and soon the great skill of this team becomes apparent. Mostly former stalkers and all veterans at the counting game, they are so experienced that their knowledge of what the deer will do is almost uncanny. All carry binoculars for general scanning and telescopes for precise identification.

The first attempt to count the Highland deer on a big scale was organized by the naturalist Frank Fraser Darling in 1953 and, since the inception of the Red Deer Commission in 1960, techniques have been progressively refined to the point at which ninety-five per cent accuracy is claimed. The possibility of counting animals twice has been almost eliminated and, if anything, the team tends to under-estimate by some five per cent.

The deer range in Scotland is so huge – nearly eight million acres – that they can tackle only part of it each year. In 1986 they managed 60,000 acres, and they reckon to cover a particular stretch of ground once every ten years. For large, flat areas holding relatively few deer, the humans are reinforced by a helicopter – and this produces excellent results, for if the aircraft remains at 600 feet or higher, the deer just lie and watch it. But at £400 an hour the cost is so great that flying has to be strictly rationed.

One great merit of the count is its impartiality. Some estates, for reasons of their own, tend to exaggerate or play down the numbers of deer on their ground; but the Commission, with no axe to grind, records exactly what it sees – and now that the season is launched the team will be out every clear day of the winter, weekends included, working through the stack of invitations from forest owners.

What the counts are showing is an inexorable build-up in numbers: even though estates are being urged to cull more heavily, the total of deer has risen to its highest ever figure of 290,000 and many areas are overstocked. This is due partly to the fall in venison prices, from 90p a pound to around 55p, caused by post-Chernobyl radiation scares, and partly to the fact that estates are nervous about reducing their breeding stock; but everyone is agreed that if we get a hard, late winter, fearful mortality will result . . .

We have reached the point which looked like a ridge from where we stood in the glen. As usual, it is not the ridge at all: beyond it lies an almost flat shelf, hidden from below. Out from a hollow in front of us bob a hind and calf. 'That's it exactly!' exclaims Dick. 'The brutes are lying in the holes. They've all to be shifted.'

True to form, the hind and calf run into the wind, then stop to look back. More hinds come up out of a burn, disturbed by the scent of the animals moving ahead of them. Soon twenty have collected into a herd. As we move forward, they go on over the top into Acky's glen. It is as if we are playing chess on a godlike scale, shunting pieces over huge distances.

At first the stalkers' terminology is confusing. Any ground not covered by snow is described as 'black', even though most of it is dun-coloured, and the patches of grass are referred to as 'greens', even though they are now sere grey and brown. To 'get' or 'bag' a lot of deer means to count them and put them out of mind.

Now I see the point of doing this operation in winter. In summer and autumn the deer frequent the high ridges and cross over them at night, so that an accurate count would be impossible. Now the snow, lying above 1,500 feet, keeps them down and confined to limited areas; besides, being already short of food, they are loath to move far.

Now Acky, going like a stag himself in the company of John Buskie, the young beanpole of a stalker from the Reay estate, has got right out to the far rim of the corrie beyond us. He has more than 200 deer in the bowl between him and us, and he manages to tip them back, counting them as they go. Whenever he transmits, we can hear him panting.

By 2.30 pm, after five hours' scrambling, we are almost in sight of our final objective – the basin behind Aultanrynie, an old shooting lodge on the shore of Loch More. Gradually the loch comes into view; beyond it looms the perfect pyramid of Ben Stack, beyond that again the shoulders of Arkle and Foinaven, mantled with snow.

The ring is closing. Our opposite numbers are coming towards us from the north, though still we cannot see them. All movements are coordinated by Louis Stewart, the Commission's senior deer officer, watching from the road 2,000 feet below. The Aultanrynie basin is full of beasts, the air full of urgent calls: 'I put ten stags your way along the face, six and four.' 'Aye, I've got them.' 'Are you seeing the beasts tucked in on the screes?' 'I have them – no bother: they're on the skyline to me.'

At last all are accounted for. As we drop back into the glen, the setting sun glows pink on the snow summits, but frost is biting. At a debriefing in the evening grand totals for the day are worked out at 338 stags, 1,122 hinds and 404 calves – nearly 2,000 animals on that one beat.

Humans can relax in the warmth of their houses, but the deer are stuck out there in the cold, and I drive south haunted by Dick Youngson's prediction. If the winter comes in hard and snow lies late, the energy balance – already poised precariously – will turn negative for the very old and the very young. If the barren hills do not yield enough calories to sustain life, up to five per cent of the adults and twenty per cent of calves will never see the spring.

Why such restraint?

Perched up a high seat in a wood soon after dawn the other morning, waiting for deer, I threw down a sandwich crust to my Labrador. The offering hit her on the backside and bounced off, whereupon she sniffed, but did not eat it.

When unconsidered trifles fall from the table in dining-room or kitchen, she has them in a flash. But here in the open, I thought, she must be more interested in taking the wind and listening for movement in the trees. She was certainly all ears and nose, and squirrels nutting in the hazel bushes made it sound as if the whole wood was on the move. But then, a few minutes later, I noticed long dribbles of saliva hanging from her mouth and, when I eventually climbed down (no deer having presented itself), she suddenly dived on the chunk of bread as if starving.

What was it that had inhibited her from eating it before? A sense of duty – that she was on guard, and thought she could not afford to relax her vigilance? The idea seems very far-fetched, but *something* had put a powerful hex on the crust.

Such human behaviour

'We became animals,' said one of the British football hooligans being prosecuted in Belgium – as if that somehow atoned for his behaviour. I hope that the presiding judge will point out to him clearly that the implications of his remark – that animals behave badly – are quite unfounded.

Of course carnivorous animals kill and eat other animals (as do humans), but that is what nature designed them for. What they do *not* do is get drunk, swear, fight, hate foreigners, run amok in gangs and wantonly smash things up. The more animals are studied, the clearer it becomes that their social organization is in many ways superior to that of humans.

The point is put perfectly in the last act of Mozart's *The Marriage of Figaro*. With all the characters in a frenzy of sexual jealousy, frustration and intrigue, Marcellina sings her lovely, sinuous aria *Il capro e la capretta*. The goat and his mate never carry on like *this*, she says. Even the most ferocious wild creatures live in harmony, and it is only we poor humans who inflict such cruelty on each other.

Life on my dream estate

Perusing a list of the country's leading millionaires – those with £10 million or more to their names – I was wafted gently into the realms of my favourite fantasy.

I own 10,000 acres, rising from sea level to heather-clad moors. The low ground is good land and heavily afforested, the woods containing both roe and fallow deer. My house, in the centre of the estate, is naturally a Queen Anne jewel, not too big, commanding extensive views and goods fields of fire to all points of the compass.

Having millions in the bank, I do not require the estate to produce a vast return and I can, therefore, afford to run it in a way that benefits all its elements – humans, livestock, wildlife and the environment itself. I do not need the Government to tell me to grow less corn; I cut down on artificial fertilizers years ago, and most of my arable fields are already bounded by six-yard headlands of grass, which link together to form long-distance bridleways with strongly-built jumps let into the fences at appropriate points so that riders can get up speed across country.

Walkers are admirably provided with footpaths, stiles and gates –

but I do not kowtow to those officious bodies which seek to assert their rights in the face of all reason. I point out to their representatives that, whereas in the old days paths were created to link one farm or village with the next by the shortest route, the people who walk them today are not trying to get from A to B as fast as possible: rather they are seeking fresh air and exercise in agreeable surroundings, so that now and then they can perfectly well go round a field rather than straight across it.

On the farm I use weed-killers and insecticides as little as possible; in any case I follow the guidelines pioneered by the Game Conservancy and do not spray right to the edges of my crops. This restraint, reinforced by the existence of the grass headlands, has given me the highest grey partridge count of any estate in England. We do not rear any partridges or pheasants, but I do employ a gamekeeper to control vermin and run a shoot reputed to show the highest birds in England.

My 2,000 acres of forestry – which fortunately escaped the October hurricane – consist mainly of hardwoods with oak, beech and ash predominating. I am lucky enough to own some spectacularly ancient oaks, which almost certainly were standing when the Spanish Armada came. Of course our aim is to preserve these giants for as long as possible.

We wage ceaseless war on grey squirrels and so keep bark-stripping of young trees to a minimum in early summer; and by selective culling we hold the deer numbers to an acceptable level as well as improving the stock. The hunt is welcome, especially later in the season, and holds its annual point-to-point on one corner of my ground. In other words, all traditional rural activities are encouraged on my land.

We process a good deal of our own timber in the saw-mill. Oak we season under cover for a minimum of five years, and we can even produce beams with a cross-section twelve inches square for the authentic restoration of local houses. We also turn out fence- and gate-posts, and rails of split larch and chestnut. My particular pride is a system of fencing that needs no nails: the rails slide through slots in the posts and lock themselves end to end, so as to present a particularly even appearance.

We also have one wood given over largely to education and entertainment. Scouts and Guides camp there. There is a nature-study, outdoor centre, fully equipped, for hire at a minimal charge. A forest walk leads to a viewing platform set above a glade, where the deer come out to feed. At the western end, where the beech dies out into thorny scrub, fifty acres have been let go as a wilderness research area.

Yet perhaps my most important social contribution has been in the village, where most of the houses used to belong to me. We are, thank God, too far from any conurbation for commuters to be a threat, but for years I have run a benevolent scheme which makes it possible for ordinary people to live here, and protects them against the pernicious influence of outsiders with more money.

Not merely in the environs of cities, but all along the motorways that radiate from them, I hear of villages being wrecked as house prices rocket, city slickers move in and ordinary folk are driven away, leaving half the dwellings owned by weekenders, who have no time or inclination to show any interest in the community.

That does not happen here. I do from time to time sell a house, but only with a signed agreement to the effect that if the buyer later wants to move on, he or she must sell it back to the estate at a price deemed reasonable by an independent tribunal. The house then goes on the market again, but on the same terms, so that firm control is maintained. Prices, in consequence, are thirty per cent lower than on the open market; first-time buyers get a good start and a reasonable return when they move away, but they cannot make huge killings. The result is that traditional families have stayed in place, the community is thriving and our cricket team beats hell out of all comers. I need hardly add that the old ale from our local brewery is sought out from fifty miles afield.

Of course not everything is perfect: life would be deadly if it were. One must always have a project – and my latest is to pioneer a system of geo-thermal heating that will service the entire community. Already we have one or two hot springs in the neighbourhood, and seismic surveys suggest that deep exploration would yield startling results. Free heat for the whole village in perpetuity? Why not? If Iceland can do it, surely we can too.

And where is this idyllic place? At the moment, alas, it exists only in my head. But I am sure that if a cheque for £20 million – correction, £30 million – landed in my letter-box tomorrow, I should start looking for a suitable estate after breakfast and make its continual improvement my life's work.

In praise of rabies rules

Used as we are to outbursts of agricultural noise (and language), we paid no particular attention when a commotion erupted from the direction of the village. Although silence usually reigns, there is often the snarl of a chain-saw, the bellow of a cow or the grinding of a tractor to entertain the ear. This was obviously a dog fight, and a good one: an explosion of yapping and barking, reinforced by terrific human roars. Fair enough, I thought: somebody breaking up a canine difference of opinion – and I went on sharpening my slasher for an assault on our bottom hedge.

The set-to had been more serious than I realized. A few minutes later there appeared at the edge of our field a boy of about eighteen, dripping with blood from punctures in hands, wrists and face. He was in a state of shock and barely able to describe what had happened, but the gist of it was that his own little white mongrel – part Corgi, part terrier – which he was taking for a walk, had suddenly been attacked by a Golden Retriever.

Fearing for his dog's life, he made the very substantial mistake of bending down to pick it up. At once he was caught by a flurry of bites – probably from both combatants – and by the time he had hoisted the mongrel to safety, he was in a mess, with holes all round his chin as well as in his hands. Luckily he needed no stitches, and I do not think he will be permanently disfigured; my wife cleaned up his wounds and took him off to get an anti-tetanus jab from the doctor. The dog, of course, was scarcely marked, protected by its tough, loose skin. All the same, it too had been punctured here and there.

The one certain result is that its owner will never make that mistake a second time. If Fido ever gets into another fight, he will set about the assailant with stick or boot, and drive it off that way. But he had a nasty fright, and the incident left me thinking, yet again, how marvellously fortunate we are not to have rabies in these islands.

Had rabies been endemic in our foxes – as it is over wide stretches of Europe – the boy would not have escaped so lightly. He did not know where the Retriever had come from, and when, after the fight, it ran off, he was too shaken to notice which way it had gone. It may have been one of the village dogs, but equally it may have belonged to a visitor. In any case, suppose efforts to trace it had failed – what then?

To be safe, both the boy and his mongrel would have needed immediate vaccination. One jab would have sufficed for the dog, but the boy would have needed a course of six, given in his arms on days 0, 3, 7, 14, 30 and 90 after the attack. Besides, the wounds in his chin would have been particularly dangerous. The bullet-shaped rabies virus travels up the nerve fibres to the brain and, when someone is bitten in the head, it has only a short way to go. Almost certainly, therefore, he would have been injected with special anti-rabies immunoglobulin right into the face wounds. His experience, unpleasant anyway, would have turned into a nightmare, for it would have put him and his family under severe psychological stress, leaving them to face months of worry, uncertain (in spite of doctors' reassurances about the efficacy of the vaccine) that he was going to be all right.

I am profoundly glad that our authorities – principally the Ministry of Agriculture and H.M. Customs – make such strenuous efforts to keep rabies out of Britain. Yet at the same time I cannot see why they are now paying so little regard to developments in West Germany, where scientists working under the auspices of the World Health Organization have had great success with a vaccine which immunizes foxes, the main vectors of the disease.

By distributing vast numbers of fish-meal baits containing vaccine capsules –five million so far – the Germans have managed to clear huge areas of rabies altogether and they are confident that, given enough money and cooperation from neighbours, they could rid all western Europe of the scourge. To anyone who works in the countryside or has shooting dogs (for example), it is an immense relief not to have to worry any longer about the risk of being contaminated.

Yet in Britain the Ministry of Agriculture persists with its old-fashioned plans for dealing with an outbreak, should one occur: the aim would be to kill as many foxes as possible within the immediate area by the deployment of baits laced with strychnine. Would it not be less dangerous to bomb the area with vaccine, rather than with poison, and immunize local foxes instead of trying to wipe them out?

Death of a hunter

I was sad to find a buzzard lying dead on the steep hillside above which I had often seen it or its fellows soaring. By ruffling back its feathers, I could tell from the absence of wounds that it had not been shot and, from the way its feet were stretched rigidly out behind it, I reckoned that it must have been poisoned.

I should have sent it for a *post mortem*, but it so happened that the nearest man who could have carried out an examination was going on holiday that day and, although I could have put the body into the deep-freeze against his return, I somehow never got round to it. Perhaps, deep down, I did not really want to know the cause of death. There are no gamekeepers near us, and nobody (I hope) is waging a campaign against hawks. I would like to think the buzzard died by accident, having eaten a rat made sleepy by legitimate poisoning.

Even in death it was a formidable bird: its curved beak and talons needle-sharp, its dark eyes of a commanding size. Already another pair are soaring high above the slope where its days ended. They, having no conception of death, are preparing to nest and getting on with life; but whenever I hear their piercing whistles ring down the valley, I cannot help thinking of the one that has gone.

Expletive not deleted

I should love a professor of semantics – perhaps a visiting American – to spend a week or two in our neighbourhood studying local use of the words 'bugger' and 'buggery'. Before anyone takes offence, let me hasten to say that I have never yet heard either spoken in its literal, physical sense down our way. Nor, I should add, have they any connection with – though they are phonetically indistinguishable from – the Hindustani word *bhagar*, meaning a low-lying, marshy watercourse. Rather, they are put to continuous use in a variety of metaphorical applications.

Some, of course, are by no means confined to our area. 'Well, I'm buggered!' indicates consternation, as it does anywhere else, and the simple 'I'm buggered' means 'I'm exhausted', just as 'Buggered if that ain't' means 'Of course it is'. 'Bugger off' and 'bugger all' speak for themselves.

Beyond these commonplaces, however, extend a variety of special invocations. For instance, the noun often indicates extremes, not necessarily good or bad. Thus in summer the weather is sometimes said to be 'hot as buggery', and in winter 'cold as buggery'. A poodle appearing on television at Cruft's dog show is described by the farmer (derisively) as 'spruced up to buggery', and the cricket ball which had to be exhumed from the midriff of Cyril, the square-leg umpire, was 'going like buggery'.

The French tourist, inquiring politely of a likely looking fellow at the Sun Inn, 'You are the landlord, yes?', is neither pleased nor enlightened to receive the explosive retort, 'Am I buggery!' (Or even, 'I am buggery!') He suspects that something rude has been said, but he is not sure what.

Often the word has distinctly disparaging overtones – as when a gamekeeper refers savagely to his former employer (a titled lady) as 'the Old Bugger'. But equally, it can mean something desirable. 'Won't that be a bugger if she goes!' said Bob, the blacksmith, enthusiastically as we struggled with a defunct tractor. 'Won't it, eh?'

Perhaps the subtlest application is when the word is used like some special Latin adverb (cf *nonne* or *num*) to mean 'No, on the contrary.' Thus at the climax of a narration about Lizzie, the village tart, who explained a suspiciously long absence to her mother by saying she had been to choir practice in church, the question, '*Had* she?' is roundly despatched by, 'Bugger! She bin shaggin' in the bus shelter.' In this case the word is uttered in a slightly cracked tone suggestive of incredulity and derision.

Our American professor would have a good deal to get on with, I think. But there is one essential precondition: women's lib notwithstanding, our academic would have to be a man, for in female company eloquence deserts the locals. Denied the words that oil the wheels of everyday discourse, they become tongue-tied and incoherent.

Action on smelling a rat

I am glad to report that the ongoing Dead Rat Situation has at last been resolved – though not without the expenditure of quite some nervous and physical energy. The trouble began a couple of days after my wife had gone off on a short holiday. When I opened the door of the room in which she works, I noticed a strange and musty smell. 'Damp,' I thought – so I lit the wood-burning stove and closed the door.

The only effect of heat was to increase the smell disastrously. After another couple of days things had become so noisome that I felt it necessary to call in outside advisers. Women tended to ascribe the stink to rising damp, men to something dead. It was the gamekeeper who put me on the right lines. 'It's a bloody rat,' he announced confidently. 'Course it is. Under the floorboards.'

Fearing the worst – that the whole floor would have to come up – I loosed the dogs into the stricken room in the hope that they would mark the quarry down, but all they did was rush about with their noses in the air, clearly saying, 'This smell is so overpowering that it is neither desirable nor necessary to pinpoint its source too closely.'

There was nothing for it but to start having the floorboards up. By a miracle, the first hole I cut proved to be in almost exactly the right place. There, only one joist away, lay the source of the fumes. A rat it was – or had been, now not so much decomposing as deliquescing. As I lifted it carefully with a pair of fire-tongs, various barely mentionable pieces, possibly once limbs, fell away and had to be retrieved individually. One by one I clawed them up and put them in a bucket.

One new floorboard, cut to size, restored the *status quo* indoors; one new airbrick secured the external defences. But I shall never forget the smell, which I can only describe as *grey* and suggestive of very old witches.

This account prompted Mrs Mary Lucas of New Malden to send in the following splendid remedy, taken from a book called *Labour-Saving Hints and Ideas for the Home*, published in 1924: 'To locate a dead rat in a room, catch half-a-dozen bluebottle flies and slip them into a glass jar. Let the flies out in the room where you suspect the rat is and sit down whilst they fly around. Within an hour they will have scented the rat and all be buzzing round one spot. That is where your rat is. You can then take up the board and remove the pest.'

So now I know. There are only two snags. One is that I am not too well versed in the catching of bluebottles. Swatting, yes. Spraying, certainly. But trapping? Would it not be rather a slow business? The other problem is that bluebottles hibernate and are, therefore, not available for duty in winter.

It was usually in winter that the dead rat menace struck those doughty writers Somerville and Ross (authors of *The Irish R.M.* among other jewels). Drishane, their home in County Cork, was rat-infested and, when they put down poison, rodents succumbed in hideous numbers beneath the floors. One night in November 1878 the stench in the dining-room became so bad that they were forced to eat elsewhere, and on 1 December 1890 Edith Somerville wrote in her diary of 'awful smells in the billiard room'. Having dealt with one rat only, I know she did not exaggerate.

Positively the final word on this topic: a wry reminiscence from a friend who owns a substantial and ancient house far up a valley in the Welsh mountains, and got married rather late in life to a girl a good deal younger than himself.

After their honeymoon the couple settled down at home, but soon began to be troubled by an elusive yet pernicious smell in the bathroom. Being newly wed and not yet used to living with a partner, neither liked to say anything for fear of giving offence. Though hardly able to believe it, each began to suspect that the other must have some unmentionable habit which left this gradually increasing stink behind.

Eventually the problem reached such proportions as to overpower politeness. Investigation revealed you-know-what – and the tension that had been building up was immediately relieved. But the rotting rodent, reinforced by an excess of courtesy, had brought the marriage perilously close to disaster.

A question of when is a goat

In northern Norway the other day I came across a creature entirely new to me. Admittedly it was stuffed and in the lobby of a hotel, but still it gave me a jolt – a lithe, low, powerful-looking predator about four feet long, like a giant pine-marten.

When my host told me it was a goat-bear and much hated by farmers because it killed sheep, I felt doubtful. But I bit back a sceptical answer – and now I am glad, for a check reveals that the animal must have been a wolverine, which does take sheep, and in winter can kill deer because of its superior speed over deep snow.

The incident reminded me of an occasion when, as literary editor in charge of that formidable critic Dame Rebecca West, I printed a book review in which she lambasted the author for writing about goats that climbed trees. Rising to majestic heights of indignation, Dame Rebecca came down gloriously, loosing off sarcastic broadsides about credulity in general and zoological ignorance in particular.

The effect was magnificent. But alas, for once she was absolutely wrong. Not only did several readers write in to say that goats often climb trees: one sent in a photograph showing Billy high in the branches, and our humiliation was complete.

Call of the jungle

'Is that the one what screeches so 'orrible?' asked Mavis, a regular in the public bar. As it happened she was trying to identify a pop singer, but she might just as well have been referring to our peacock, who, with the pressures of a new mating season upon him, has once again hit top vocal form.

The trouble is that he takes every sound produced by the environment as a threat or insult and feels constrained to drown it in decibels. No matter that a noise may be perfectly innocuous – provided it breaks the silence suddenly, it sets him off. A distant jet, a power-saw starting up half a mile away, a dog barking, a car passing in the lane, one human calling to another – any excuse is good enough for a penetrating blast of 'ay-orr'.

Occasionally I have hopes that he is going to lose his voice, for sometimes in mid-cry it cracks into a hoarse roar; but I fear his vocal cords are made of titanium (that is certainly how they sound) and always seem to recover after a few minutes' rest. If one succumbs to irritation and starts to count the number of times he lets fly, the morning rapidly becomes intolerable.

Yet there is one note of comfort in the cacophony: he has recently

begun to answer the telephone. If he can be trained to respond selectively to the sound of the bell and broadcast a riposte over the fields when we are working outside, he will be of real service.

Field-sports, unlimited

In March, as everyone knows, hares are supposed to go mad. Certainly they race about extravagantly and also sit up boxing with their front feet, but until now the reasons for such behaviour have remained largely mysterious. I was, therefore, delighted to learn about Tony Holley, the Somerset solicitor who has spent 1,500 hours studying hares and has discovered some illuminating new facts about them. He has found, for instance, that when one boxes another, it is the female which indulges in fisticuffs – to drive off an importunate jack – rather than one male battling with another for a female, as has always been thought.

Yet it is not Mr Holley's findings which fascinate me, so much as his research apparatus. This consists of a 300-power astronomical telescope, mounted in the roof of his house, whose magnification is such that it enables him to observe and recognize individual animals several thousand yards off.

From the thought of a country solicitor twiddling knobs in his roof-space to spy on hares five or six fields away, the mind progresses easily to extravagant fantasies of what one might arrange in the way of special facilities or equipment for field-sports if one had unlimited funds. For instance, if you owned a Scottish deer forest and wished to escape the indignity and discomfort of having to crawl across exposed areas when approaching your quarry, you would obviously have the whole mountain excavated into a grid-square of ditches, along which you could move unseen without even having to bend down.

Nearer home, I see myself at the controls of equipment similar to, but rather more elaborate than, that of Mr Holley. On the roof, in a weatherproof housing, a television camera fitted with an image-intensifier for night vision. Coupled to it, a high-velocity rifle. Down below, in the control room, each wall a television screen, depicting that quarter of the compass. A joy-stick coupled to the central computer enables me to pan and tilt the camera so that I can scrutinize the fields round about. One press of a switch on the stick superimposes the cross-hairs of the rifle-sight on the screen, so that, with absolute precision, I can take out incoming targets such as foxes making for the lambs or the poultry. A secondary armament firing anaesthetic darts is excellent for immobilizing human marauders ...

But I seem to have come rather a long way from my starting point, which was the harmless and attractive mad March hare.

A dump in a million

Let me introduce you to the delights of our local rubbish tip. You think I am being sarcastic? Not at all. The place is so well run that every visit to it is a pleasure.

For a start, it is admirably sited on top of a hill, commanding views of open country to all points of the compass. At nearly 800 feet above sea level, the air is particularly bracing: that is to say, there is usually a howling wind, which whips away any smells that might lurk about in more sheltered spots.

The place is under the general supervision of a huge Alsatian, whose coat is so furry that he is quite at home out of doors in all but the harshest weather. He is generally on station by the Portakabin office at the gate, at ease on his rug and equipped with a football in case a lull in the flow of patrons should leave him with time on his paws.

He is flanked on either side by well-tilled flower beds and stretches of neat lawn. In winter the flowers tend to be plastic – chrys-anthemums rooted in six inches of snow present a striking appear-ance – but in summer they are real enough, and there is not a weed to be seen. A strong show of polystyrene gnomes, toadstools and old boots adds tone to the horticulture.

This is in the hands of the dog's master. On paper he is the council's manager, but I think of him as the owner of the whole establishment, for it is he who has raised the site to its present standard, and he has a distinctly proprietorial air. In any case, he is certainly the boss. It was his training in the Brigade of Guards, he will tell you, that gave him his passion for tidiness, and there is not one scrap of paper or bottle-top out of place. Anyone careless enough to spill or drop something is immediately offered a broom and shovel with which to clear up the mess.

The amenities include bottle-banks, tanks for old oil, a special bin for metal, and – glory of glories – the crusher, which swallows and compacts domestic rubbish with gargantuan voracity. Since the site is an old quarry, in the bottom of which springs rise, nothing toxic is dumped here for fear of contaminating the water-table, and almost all the refuse is taken away for disposal at one of the council's main tips elsewhere.

Hence the crusher. Whenever the bin is nearly full, the boss steps forward and performs his magic ritual. Motors whirr, steel doors close and the bin descends to a lower level, where, from one side, a ram applies irresistible force (forty-four tons, in fact) to the unspeakable assembly within, compacting it into twelve-ton lumps. The result is that only one or two loads have to be taken away each day, rather than dozens.

Not surprisingly, use of the service is brisk. A normal weekday brings in about a hundred cars, but on Saturdays, when people tackle their gardens, the number rises to 400 – a continuous procession of vehicles coming and going. Nothing is refused, provided it is of domestic origin: ruptured mattresses, burnt-out cookers, mowing machines that have blown their top – all are received with equanimity and consigned unchallenged to their doom.

Quite apart from dumping rubbish of my own, I find it instructive to hang about and observe the faces of other customers. They arrive looking strained and furtive, clearly afraid that their horrible rejects (which they have done their damnedest to disguise) are going to be turned away. But as soon as they see them descend safely into the maw of the crusher, their demeanour lights up, and suddenly they are full of chat and banter.

Heady price of a sunshine bargain

All I wanted on that day of brilliant sunshine was a few screws. 'Twenty of those, please,' I said to the boy in the hardware shop, 'and twenty of these.' As he was counting them, my eye fell once more on the wheelbarrow parked invitingly outside the door. It was green and black, compact – and it glistened in the sun. On my way in I had half noticed that it was on offer, knocked down from £37 to £30.

The boy kept counting, dropping the screws into little brown paper bags, on which he scribbled the price. With three barrows on the farm already, we did not exactly need another, but all our existing ones had various drawbacks . . .

'That the lot then?' said the boy.

'Just some of these. Ten'll do.'

At the till the girl rang up the scribbled totals. 'Eleven pounds exactly,' she said.

'*What?* Are you sure that's right?'

She checked, and of course it was right. But just as I was feeling outraged to be paying £11 for a few screws, I heard someone who sounded dreadfully like me saying, 'I'll take that wheelbarrow too.' So suddenly I found myself writing a cheque for £41.

The boy came out with me. 'You can have one flat, if you like,' he said. He was trying to be helpful and could not have known that I would find his offer perfectly maddening. I had got the impression – fostered, no doubt, by the careful positioning of the exhibit – that my barrow was the only one of its kind. Now, too late, I realized that there were probably dozens of them, not even assembled, in the store.

'It's quite all right,' I said. 'I'll have it as it is.' And I wheeled it furiously away with the screws dumped inside.

It's the sunshine, I kept telling myself on the way home. It's this diamond-bright day that is to blame. I am glad to report that at home the barrow received an enthusiastic welcome, and by now I have almost managed to persuade myself that it was a bargain. But I shall take care to wait for a thoroughly miserable morning before I go buying screws again.

❧

One up for Chas the brewer

It is always good for morale when one of us rustics manages to score off a huge urban bureaucracy, but rarely does anyone manage to land such a well-placed kick as that recently planted in the vitals of H.M. Customs and Excise by Chas Wright, the Falstaffian brewer of Uley in Gloucestershire.

In less than two years Chas has established such a wide reputation for his village ales that Old Spot and Pig's Ear (both lethal brews) are in keen demand as far afield as Oxford, some fifty miles away. Like all brewers, he pays beer duty to H.M. Customs and Excise by means of a well-established system of post-dated cheques. Thus, the duty for March will be paid by a cheque sent off in the middle of April and dated April 25. The agreed delay is a concession by the Excise, which in effect gives brewers three extra weeks' interest on their money. The beermakers use the system gratefully and are careful not to default on payments, because, if they do, the Excise has power to change the locks on their premises, seize their equipment and even close them down.

Chas was, therefore, considerably startled when, in the hazy run-up to Christmas, he received a letter from Miss B. Evans of H.M. Customs in Liverpool, which told him in peremptory terms that he had *again* been submitting currently-dated cheques, in spite of an earlier warning. (In fact he had sent one cheque, for £4,600 dated 15 December in mistake for 25 December.) This time, she said, his cheque would not be cashed immediately. 'However, if any further currently-dated cheques are received at this office, they will be cashed at once, and no further warning letter will be sent.'

This was not good enough for Chas, who rang up Miss Evans. But, when he asked, 'Would *you* mind if someone sent you your wage cheque ten days early?' she was not in the least amused, and retorted, 'That's got nothing to do with it.'

Chas, even less amused, sought the help of his local M P, Sir Anthony Kershaw, who has himself been known to lower the odd pint and who lodged a complaint with Sir Angus Fraser, Chairman of H.M. Customs, in London. Now Sir Angus has sent a handsome apology, accepting that the tone of the letter from Liverpool was 'quite inappropriate' and revealing that 'steps have been taken' to avoid any repetition.

So equilibrium has been restored in Uley Brewery; but I fancy that the evidence of Miss Evans's Christmas spirit will remain pinned on the wall for a week or two yet.

Sprightly centenarians

Who planted all the snowdrops? I do not mean those in gardens and orchards, which were obviously put there by the owner of the property; nor am I thinking of those which have been dumped in a load of garden rubbish and sprung up again (for they are amazingly resilient and will resurface even if buried beneath a foot of earth). The ones that puzzle me are those now flowering in large clumps, perhaps ten yards in diameter, way out in the middle of the woods. How did *they* come to be there?

Because they are of the double-petalled variety, which cannot be pollinated or grown from seed, it is clear that they must have been planted by humans rather than scattered by the wind. Further, they must have been planted in days when the tracks beside which they grow were walked by people with enough imagination and energy to bring about their generation. In other words, they were put there to decorate the paths which run from the village to the site of the big house on top of the hill. But since the house was demolished almost forty years ago, it follows that the snowdrops are older than that.

In my ignorance, I could not imagine why the bulbs had not gone blind after so long; but now I learn from experts that snowdrops continue flowering indefinitely – certainly for one hundred years or more – even if they are never moved or divided. Far from dying out, woodland clumps are often extended by pheasants and other birds scratching shallowly planted bulbs about. Another feature which contributes to their longevity is that they contain crystals distasteful to mice, which dine freely on crocuses but leave snowdrops alone.

Armed with this knowledge, I have come to regard the little white drifts with new admiration. What colony of human beings with a hundred winters behind them could go down flat on the ground after an unseasonably late blizzard – as the snowdrops did last weekend – and then, with the thaw, immediately come up smiling?
** After the publication of this article a neighbour pointed out that some of the snowdrop patches probably mark the sites of cottages which have disappeared. It pleases me to think that such humble plants can outlive man-made dwellings of wood and stone.

When fox meets deer

Out early after deer the other morning, I saw a sight that, even if I live to be a hundred, I am sure will never be vouchsafed to me again. I was trying to cull a particular animal – a fallow buck with a broken back leg. As dawn came up in a crimson blaze behind me, I settled into position at the edge of a field on top of the hill. The herd of deer was in range, but as usual I could not see the one I wanted.

A dry clicking noise proclaimed that two of the bucks were sparring. There they were, antlers braced together as they wrestled briefly in front of a stone wall. But suddenly, as I watched them through binoculars, I realized that there was other movement within the circle of the glass. Looking down a bit, I made out two foxes sitting at the foot of the wall, grooming each other.

Two fallow bucks and two foxes in the glass at once – it was an amazing combination. At once I began wondering whether each species took any notice of the other – and in a few moments I had an answer.

A pricket (or second-year buck) came walking along beside the wall towards me and all at once, on top of the wall just ahead of it, appeared one of the foxes, its coat glowing like ripe apricots in the first rays of the sun. The pricket, evidently puzzled, quickened its pace and began to make jabbing thrusts with its head. The fox seemed to find this amusing, for it ambled along the wall top making no effort to get away, but swishing its brush back and forth in the deer's face, just as a cat thrashes its tail when it is annoyed or excited.

How the encounter would have ended naturally, I do not know, for an eddy of wind betrayed my presence, and in a flash deer and foxes vanished. But that extraordinary glimpse made the struggle of leaving a warm bed at 5 am seem infinitely worthwhile.

Country matters?

I used to wonder how people who take holiday cottages out of season occupy their time. In summer, obviously, they go out into the country, picnic, sightsee and so on; but in winter there is very little to entertain them.

Observation, however, suggests that many come with their entertainment already well planned. I recently kept an eye on one particular cottage on and off for a week. A car standing outside marked
the couple to ground, but as far as I saw they never broke cover for
six whole days. I do not think they even opened a window or looked
out.

So now, if anyone asks me what such people are engaged in, I
reply – with a hint of interrogation – as the Prince of Denmark does
to Ophelia in Act III, Scene 2, of *Hamlet*, by suggesting, 'Country
matters?'

Herons on the warpath

Scuttling home to the village, a boy blurted out that he had been
dive-bombed by 'a great big crane'. All that had happened, in fact,
was that a heron had flown low over his head – but the incident gives
rise to agreeable visions of the tabloid headlines that would be needed
to do justice to his encounter: HERON HORROR ATTACK/HERON
TERROR SHOCK/HOCK SHERRY TERROR ...

The boy survived. Not so many of the fish in the ponds which our
neighbour has constructed in the valley. For the past few weeks they
have been under siege by a pair of herons which flight in during the
night or just as dawn is breaking. Sometimes I hear their peculiar,
rasping cries as they come over the hill, and most mornings, when I
walk along the bottom field, at least one slim, grey, fence-post-like
shape poised beside the water suddenly unfolds huge wings and
climbs laboriously away.

Since herons are a fully protected species, my neighbour can hardly
shoot the marauders, and he is too law-abiding a fellow to incite
anyone else to knock them off. Even so, I keep thinking of Willie, a
Highland ghillie and poacher, who once confided to me that,
although a 'very puir shot' with a shotgun, he had once had a great
triumph when a heron flew up the river as he crouched on the bank.
'I let drive,' he said, eyes gleaming, 'and boy – there was nothing
but a cloud of feathers!'

I feel sure that the farmer will not resort to Willie the ghillie's
methods. But how else can he protect his fish?

Already a stout and lifelike scarecrow, got up in a green boilersuit such as the farmer himself wears, has proved useless: within a couple of days of its appearance on the bank, one of the herons was strolling contemptuously past it a few feet away. The sheep-netting that surrounds the ponds is no defence, as the birds land in the field outside it and hop over. According to another neighbour, the answer would be to import one of the dummy herons – made of plastic or polystyrene, guaranteed weatherproof, and exceedingly lifelike – such as are purveyed in mail-order catalogues, the idea being that the raiders, seeing the pond already tenanted, would push off. The farmer, however, had already considered the idea and rejected it, for fear that it might have an effect exactly opposite the one intended and decoy birds in rather than scare them away. He was put off by the experience of a friend who had just such a dummy in his garden and, on looking out of the window one morning, was astonished to see a real heron thrashing wildly as it tried to copulate with the polystyrene pseud.

So now our neighbour is at a loss and the herons have a free run of the ponds. Try as I may, I cannot find it in me to like them. I have a certain admiration for their amazing shape – in the air they remind me of pterodactyls, so angular is their outline – and for the way in which evolution has adapted them to perform a particular function; but their habits are by no means attractive. They hunt by stealth, relying on immobility to lure prey within reach, and they eat not only fish – which they grab with open beak or spear – but also live frogs, water-rats and ducklings. One heron will devour a whole brood of mallard in a few minutes, and its appetite is gargantuan: although the bird is so tall, it weighs no more than three or four pounds, yet it has been known to put away fish up to fourteen inches long, weighing at least a pound and a half. In other words, it can eat half its own weight at a standing.

Provided the temperature stays above freezing, herons survive the winter very well. It is when ponds and lakes ice over that they run into trouble – and the number of breeding pairs in Britain fluctuates sharply according to the weather: from a high of some 5,000 in the 1950s, it was cut to half that by the savage winter of 1962–3.

The pair now harassing our valley are eating royally, for one of the ponds contains some Japanese *koi*, which, if you bought them in a shop, would cost several pounds apiece. Admittedly they were abandoned there by a man who had been taken short – he drove up with the fish in a bucket, on the point of expiry, and dumped them with such a rush that he did not have time to ask permission or explain his predicament – but even so, it does not seem right that herons should get such exotic fare for breakfast.

Murder at last light

Once again the dusk was rent by the scream of some creature *in extremis*. But what could have made such a harsh and desperate noise?

There was still enough light to see, through binoculars, that the peacocks were safely aloft in their tree on the edge of the wood. The chickens were securely shut into the barn. The noise had been too low and loud for a rabbit got by a stoat. Morning revealed that the victim had been a rook, snatched by a fox at the far end of our top field. Rank black feathers lay everywhere, cut off cleanly by the killer's razor teeth, but there was no sign of the body, which had no doubt been eaten when still warm. Having never tried rook myself, I do not fancy the idea – but obviously the taste is perfectly acceptable to a fox.

The debris reminded me how often one sees rooks continuing to feed on the ground, recklessly late, long after most other birds have gone to roost, particularly at this time of the year. The reason, I think, is that at the end of the winter, when there are few seeds or insects about, they have difficulty finding enough to eat, and need every minute of daylight for their search. They also need to stock up to withstand the cold of the night, and so do not head for home till the last possible moment.

I am glad to think that Shakespeare noticed this habit 400 years ago, and fixed it in Macbeth's hair-raising lines:

> Light thickens, and the crow
> Makes wing to the rooky wood;
> Good things of day begin to droop and
> drowse,
> Whiles night's black agents to their
> preys do rouse.

On not going up the wall

The hazards of redecorating an ancient farmhouse are obvious: the whole structure is leaning in various directions and nowhere in the place is there a decent right-angle, so that when one tries to match up the pattern on new paper, one is driven – as you might say – up the wall. Also, the removal of old paper or even merely of paint is liable to reveal decay far advanced.

On the other hand, there are compensations not found in newer buildings. One is that you gradually discover more about the history of the dwelling, and the other that you sometimes come on coins or other relics which have fallen down crevices in the past.

A blitz on our dining-room was disappointing in this last respect. All that turned up in the way of money – behind one wainscoting board which had rotted – was a penny and a halfpenny, both about thirty years old. Yet we also discovered that previous occupants of the house had played darts with some abandon: beneath layers of old paper on one side of the room, the plasterboard was riddled with punctures.

From the fact that a central circle was virgin, it was clear that the players had hung their dartboard without any form of surrounding and had let the wall itself take the misses. This it was well able to do, for, like most of our other walls, it is over two feet thick.

Our most substantial improvement was to replace the door leading into the kitchen. This could only be described as an abortion. The lintel, about 5′ 8″ above the floor, took unwary visitors smack in the forehead or even on the bridge of the nose, and Leslie, our excellent local builder, was dead right when he remarked on his first visit to the house, 'We shall have to higher that, shan't us?'

The door itself and the frame were horribly botched. A professional carpenter who came to instal bookshelves winced when he saw it: such barbarous workmanship, he said, made him feel positively ill. Certainly the people who were stretched out horizontally by its impact did not feel at all well.

Now the old horror has gone. The lintel has been well and truly highered, the frame rebuilt, and a new door hung. Admittedly I had to cut off the bottom panel at an angle to fit the slope of the kitchen floor, which falls like the north face of the Eiger from Aga to larder, but that is hardly a hazard to humans, and in any case it gives the new door a rakish look.

With that modest achievement behind me, I feel almost ready to tackle an altogether more ambitious project: the highering of the short passage – nay, tunnel – that leads into the sitting-room. *That* wall is all of six feet thick and to gain even a few inches of headroom will mean taking out tons of masonry. Who knows – perhaps our labours will be rewarded not merely by one or two old pennies, but by the discovery of a whole hoard immured in the massive stonework.

Fair play in the Flow Country

By removing the tax concessions which encouraged forestry in difficult terrain, the Chancellor of the Exchequer has delighted the lobby agitating against afforestation in northern Scotland, particularly the Flow Country in Caithness and Sutherland. No doubt the move was justified on a purely financial basis – for people with a great deal of money already were making more by dubious tax manoeuvres; yet it strikes me that on environmental grounds the case against establishing new woodlands in the far north has been grossly exaggerated.

The first point to be made about the Flow Country is that it is an ecological ruin – a desolate wilderness stripped of almost all life partly by overgrazing, but largely by deterioration of the climate over the millennia. Hundreds of thousands of acres, blanketed by acid peat up to twenty-five feet deep, support practically no birds or animals, such is the poverty of the vegetation.

Much is made by environmentalists of the unique nature of this colossal bog and of the birds that nest in it, especially the greenshank. Obviously the area *is* of high scientific value, yet the fact is that it harbours very few birds of any kind. When, last autumn, I spent two days there, I saw no wader of any description. Admittedly it was the wrong time of year, but even in spring people can walk for days without setting eyes on a greenshank.

The argument that new forests destroy wildlife is palpable nonsense. They do, it is true, change the texture of the ground on which they are planted, but only because the plough drains it and enables growth to begin. Besides, they cover only a relatively small area, and in any case the foresters leave alone the wettest places, which are what the waders most favour. Far from destroying, plantations positively encourage wildlife – not least mice, songbirds, hawks, owls and deer – and there is a very striking difference between the activity within a new forest and the barren wilderness outside.

Aesthetic considerations are harder to evaluate. The landscape of Caithness has a certain mournful beauty, but much of it is nearly flat and the vast, level sweeps of moorland do not rouse the spirit as do the mountains in the west. Whether or not blankets of conifers wreck the look of it is a matter of personal opinion; but the new forests are being shaped with skill and imagination, and, much as I detest conifers in most settings, my feeling is that they are less offensive here than in other places, for the landscape is so huge that it can accommodate them without detriment.

With the trees come not only new birds and wild creatures but also new jobs, new hope, a new chance to stay put for the few humans who still cling to these desolate wastes. If the Budget kills off their future, they will have no option but to seek work and homes elsewhere.

Sixty years young

Provided no more disasters strike, the 241st number of that sturdy little green-jacketed quarterly *The Countryman* will hit the bookstalls today [21 March 1987]. It seems only prudent to make the qualification, for exceptional bad luck has dogged publication of the issue which marks the magazine's sixtieth anniversary: after a fire at the regular binders', production was shifted to another firm, only for fire to break out there as well.

Such dramas have not often disturbed the even tenor of *The Countryman*'s way since it first appeared in 1927. Its founder and first editor was the redoubtable J. W. Robertson Scott, a tall, unbending teetotaller and vegetarian, invariably dressed in a tweed suit with a neatly-trimmed white mane of hair and beard, who launched the magazine from his home, Idbury Manor in Oxfordshire, when he was already sixty. Although he had been a radical journalist on the *Pall Mall Gazette* and a contributor to the *Nation*, he did not at first give his creation a very crisp sub-title, calling it 'An Illustrated Review and Miscellany of Rural Life Edited in the Country and Written by Countrymen and Countrywomen throughout the World'.

His equally formidable wife Elspet acted as co-editor, facing him across a desk, and from the start the couple solicited contributions from ordinary readers, reassuring them in the first number: 'If what you write needs any literary tinkering, we shall do all that is needed.'

The opening issue naturally carried few advertisements, but the second contained more, including announcements of two freehold cottages for sale. One, a five-bedroomed house near Stratford-upon-Avon, with ample outbuildings and an acre of orchard, was going for £700; and for the other, in an old-world village on the Essex–Herts border ('has stocks and pillory'), the owner wanted £400.

Quickly the new sapling grew into a sturdy tree. So successful was the formula – and so energetically did Robertson Scott solicit advertisements, often taking bunches of primroses and other country flowers to potential clients – that by 1939 the circulation had grown to 30,000 copies, and several of the issues were more than 400 pages long, half of them advertising. Still better, RS (as he was known) somehow managed to secure a huge stock of paper, so that he was able to escape the stringencies of wartime rationing. The result was that, when he retired in 1947 at the age of eighty, he handed on a flourishing concern.

Today the magazine is still going strong, with its circulation steady at more than 80,000, and making a healthy six-figure annual profit for its owners, United Newspapers. There were three features which the founder besought his heirs not to change – the colour of the cover, the size and the price – and it is good to see that the cover is still green, the format is the same and the price, though £1.30, is the equivalent of less than the original half-a-crown.

The magazine is now edited by Christopher Hall, a former Fleet Street man, Secretary of the Ramblers' Association and Director of the Council for the Protection of Rural England, who took over in 1981. Hock-deep in a sea of paper, he directs operations from the attic rooms of a fifteenth-century house in Burford, once a coaching inn.

The house belongs to the magazine and one of its main attractions is the amazingly long garden, which stretches away up the hill behind. A standing invitation to pay a visit is extended to all readers and every summer about a thousand take advantage of it, coming in through the archway from Sheep Street to wander or be led up the garden path.

One feels that old RS would approve of *The Countryman* sixty years on. It still offers a rich rural mixture of professional and amateur writing – unsolicited contributions pour in at the rate of twenty a day – and although it has sharpened its edge on topical matters such as conservation, it is deeply conservative in content.

Mr Hall has found to his cost that innovation does not go down well. When he decided to drop the age-old feature 'Tail Corn' – a page of short, amusing anecdotes, which he found difficult to drum up – there was such an outcry that he was forced to reinstate it. Now he openly recycles gems first printed forty years ago, and everyone is happy.

Pleasures of egg-hunting

The arrival of some new pullets immediately prompts the question: will they turn out high or low layers? In my experience, all chickens fall into one category or the other. In making nests, most seek out secret, secluded corners, comfortable and dark, but fairly low down; yet a few high-flyers choose altogether more ambitious and open sites on tops of barn walls or bale stacks, as far from the ground as they can go.

There is no better way of entertaining – that is to say, getting rid of – visiting children than to send them on an egg-hunt; the discovery of clean, brown eggs nestling in a scoop of hay or straw is immensely satisfying to almost everyone. Yet hens display astonishing ingenuity in concealing their clutches; some do not give themselves away by cackling, and at least once a year we are amazed by the emergence of a mother and family from a nest whose existence we never suspected.

Once, returning from a long spell abroad, I quizzed the family who had been in charge. Had they been getting all the eggs? 'Oh yes,' they said. 'There are four nests – A, B, C and D – but we've been keeping them empty.' Hardly had they left when a search revealed six further nests, untenanted, but containing a total of almost 150 eggs, and three hens sitting on other huge clutches.

On another occasion, I despatched a pack of small visitors to the farmyard with instructions to collect all the eggs they could find, promising 10p for every one over a dozen. I thought I knew my nests and settled down with the rest of the parents for a peaceful drink. Back came the children with fifty eggs. Some of them were old enough to have gladdened the heart of a Chinese chef; but since I had been foolish enough not to specify fresh eggs, I felt morally bound to pay.

Pied pipers of Harrods

I must confess to some disappointment at not having secured an invitation to that most coveted event of the sporting year, the Harrods rat-shoot, which takes place on its traditional date, 1 April. I had hoped that certain overtures made at other shoots during the winter might have borne fruit . . . but it was not to be. Since only seven guns can be accommodated, it is a signal honour to be invited, and a reflection no less of one's reputation as a shot than of one's social standing.

The shoot is held in the Harrods cellars, which extend for acres, not only under the store itself and beneath Brompton Road, but up under Trevor Square and Knightsbridge and into the bowels of Hyde Park. Guests are expected to wear grey, and in recent years it has become fashionable to have a plus-four suit of lightweight grey Loden made for the occasion.

On arrival – at 6.45 for 7 am – one is greeted by the Head Cellarer in plum-coloured velvet and taken to the gun-room to select a weapon. The armoury contains 15 double-barrelled .410 ejectors, with stocks of various lengths (two of them are cast-off for left-handers). These light and perfectly-balanced weapons were made to special order by Holland & Holland in 1912, but since they are used only once a year, and well maintained, they remain in mint condition. Guests can choose cartridges loaded with No. 8 or No. 9 shot, but most opt for the finer No. 9.

After traditional preliminaries, which include a glass of Buck's fizz, the usual draw for places, and the issue of pellet-proof gaiters, the shoot begins in the far north-west corner of the ground, each block of about an acre being driven – as in a pheasant shoot – with five guns forward and two back.

Until recently, the beaters were accompanied by terriers, but now that most goods are stored on pallets (which give excellent cover to the rats, but are too low for dogs to penetrate), the men are furnished with electronic goads, which push the quarry forward with high-frequency pulses. This sets up a squeaking such as the Pied Piper never evoked, and generates great excitement. In the firing line, speed, dexterity and coolness are everything, for by the time the rats cross the narrow open spaces between blocks, they are travelling fast and offer only fleeting chances.

There are three different teams of beaters, so that one drive can succeed another without delay. Block by block, the cellars are brought into the final drive – the area used for storage of cereals, where the rats are encouraged to congregate. In a good year, such as this promises to be, the bag should amount to nearly 200 head.

In the old days the victims used to be conveyed by horse-drawn carriage to Regent's Park for the delectation of the inmates of the Reptile House; but now that the dangers of lead-poisoning are more fully understood, the bodies are incinerated. At Harrods itself, pro-ceedings close with a breakfast of salmon kedgeree, vodka and fresh peaches in the proprietors' suite on the top floor.

It would, of course, be possible to control the vermin by modern, chemical means, and every time the store has changed hands in recent years, there have been fears in the sporting fraternity that the shoot might give way to Warfarin and rodent operatives. Happily, each new set of owners has opted to maintain tradition – and none more enthusiastically than the Al Fayed brothers, whose sporting instincts can perhaps be traced to their distant background in the desert.

The origins of the event are uncertain, but it certainly goes back more than a hundred years, and probably almost to the foundation of Harrods in 1849. Unfortunately, very little has appeared in print about the shoot, for Victorian and Edwardian sporting authors considered any reference to it infra dig.

Thus the great purist Sir Ralph Payne-Gallwey never mentioned it (deriding it in private as 'one of the most contemptible manifestations of the *rus in urbe* school'), but the sixth Earl of Walsingham – who was invited in the spring of 1879 after setting the record of 1,070 grouse to his own gun in one day the previous autumn – could not refrain from some mild boasting in his memoirs. The time is surely ripe for a social historian to give this unique event the treatment it calls for.

Backstage at Badminton

How would *you* like to have the grounds of your house overrun by a quarter of a million people? Not much, I imagine; and it seems to me that the eleventh Duke of Beaufort looks upon the spring invasion of Badminton – which starts on Thursday – with commendable equanimity.

Admittedly his establishment is rather larger than yours or mine: the house has 'about forty bedrooms'; the park surrounding it 350 gently undulating acres, and the estate 20,000. At least there is plenty of space. Nevertheless, the impact of the annual horse trials can be devastating.

Last year, for instance, it rained so catastrophically that on the final day cars had to be banned altogether – but not before other vehicles and the fifteen tractors dragging them out had reduced the place to a quagmire.

The present Duke, who succeeded to the title four years ago, is himself no mean rider, having come second in the trials on Countryman in 1959, and as president he takes a keen professional interest in the running of the three-day event. He has thus, with slightly different emphasis, carried on the tradition set by his predecessor and cousin, the tenth Duke (always known as Master), who was a close friend of the Queen and used to have members of the Royal Family to stay.

The new landlord still throws a cocktail party for 800 participants and organizers, and puts up all the grooms in the stable block, where they not only live free but also eat free, getting four excellent meals a day.

Inevitably the character of the event has changed since its inception in 1949. Gone are the days when Master would throw his jacket over a bale of straw for the Queen to sit on. The inexorable build-up of numbers has rendered such informality impossible.

Old-timers lament the fact that the crowds prevent them from getting a close view of the cross-country fences, and say that the whole thing isn't the fun it used to be. But that does not stop the hordes pouring in, even with a car-pass costing £7 on ordinary days and £14 for the cross-country day on Saturday, and Badminton is firmly established as the world's most celebrated three-day event.

The organizing power behind it is the redoubtable Colonel Frank Weldon, who won on Kilbarry in 1956, and for the past twenty years he has been devising ever more fiendish obstacles on the cross-country course. Now seventy, he refers to himself as 'the old fool with the bald head' and laces his explanations with invective, by no means all of it printable.

His aim, he says, is to terrify the riders but to make sure that no horse gets damaged. He points out that, although modern horses cannot run a single mile an hour faster or jump an inch higher than their ancestors of two centuries ago, human performance is continually being extended and improved.

Two years back he produced an obstacle called the Fairbanks Bounce which many entrants considered unjumpable. 'They said it was bound to kill the lot of them,' he recalls cheerfully. 'But of course it didn't bloody well kill anybody. Every single year, before the event starts, I become a personal enemy of most of the people taking part. But then, as soon as they've got round the course, they all begin saying, "How well my horse went!", and they come and congratulate me.'

It may be that the Colonel's gruff manner puts some people off at first. 'I don't want any of you buggers peering in the Duke's windows,' he says, to male and female alike, as he gives the riders their marching orders. 'And don't let your horses graze the bloody daffodils down the drive.' But they come to realize that his serious ambition is to help produce riders of Olympic standard, and in this he has been conspicuously successful.

Even Colonel Weldon admits that, for some of the people who come, the horses are not everything. 'I believe that in the suburbs you have things called car-boot sales,' he says, 'where people come and buy things? We have that here, too.'

He is referring to the trade stands, a phenomenon on their own. Such is the competition among firms to set up shop in the tented avenues that 250 companies are now on the waiting list; and since only about ten new ones gain access each year, some will still be out in the cold at the start of the twenty-first century.

It seems that some form of collective lunacy relieves people of their fiscal senses when they gather in large numbers to enjoy themselves in the open air. 'The business we do is quite phenomenal,' says Sydney Diggory, the managing director of Cambrian Fly Fishers, leading purveyors of outdoor clothes. 'I shall be extremely disappointed if I don't sell a thousand pairs of moleskin trousers in four days next week.'

At least Mr Diggory's customers are country people with practical needs. As he says, 'They're a breed of their own, and they need tough, hard-wearing pants.' Others, however, are in search of more exotic goods – and they can buy anything from smoked salmon (which is shifted by the ton) to a BMW.

All the shopkeepers agree that trade increases sharply when members of the Royal Family are present. They say that if Princess Anne, for instance, passes by, it definitely raises the tempo.

The spectators least prone to fits of financial irresponsibility are the deer – 375 of them, red and fallow – which are corralled for the duration into a much smaller area of the park than they normally enjoy. Yet sometimes the occasion goes to their heads as well. Nowadays they are physically fenced in, but on one memorable evening in the 1960s the whole lot charged across the front of the house before escaping down the drive into the surrounding woods. It took a huge cordon formed of all the estate staff – reinforced at one point by Master and the Queen Mother, who drove out after dinner – to persuade the herd to come home.

** In the event, the 1987 horse trials had to be cancelled because of incessant rain.

Keep quiet, keep still

Many thousand people will go walking in the country this Easter weekend, but few will see much in the way of wildlife for two reasons. One is that they make far too much noise, and the other that they keep moving.

The virtues of silence hardly need mentioning, although they are usually ignored, especially by children, who are often excited by the great outdoors, if not positively afraid of it, and shriek like fiends to let off steam or keep goblins at bay. But the advantages of immobility, though less obvious, are no less real.

If you walk straight through a wood, you may well conclude that there are no animals in it. In fact eyes are watching you from high and low, and it is only because wild creatures themselves use immobility as a form of protection that you do not spot them.

The most striking demonstration of this I ever saw was given by an old fallow buck one autumn. Having crawled to the edge of a rutting-stand at first light, I picked out an inferior animal and shot it. The boom of the rifle produced a general rush for safety as the rest of the deer took off.

All but one. The master buck, made wise by a lifetime's experience of escape and evasion, never moved. I knew he was there, in the middle of a clump of hazel, because I had seen him before; and presently, through the binoculars, I could again make out the curve of his neck, the sweep of one antler. I daresay his eyeballs were swivelling as he sought the source of the explosion, but otherwise, for a quarter of an hour, he shifted not a millimetre, and to the naked eye he was invisible, a 200-lb animal made part of the tracery of the forest.

Sit still yourself on a vantage-point among the trees and soon you will see how movement catches the eye to betray a creature's presence. After a few minutes the place will come alive as deer, squirrels, rabbits, hedgehogs, mice and birds resume whatever activities they were engaged in before you disturbed them. At once the wood becomes ten times as interesting; even better, you begin to feel its heartbeat, as Wordsworth did:

> One impulse from a vernal wood
> May teach you more of man,
> Of moral evil and of good,
> Than all the sages can.

Walk, then, by all means; but also, every now and then, imitate the buck. Freeze for a while and see what a spell of immobility will reveal.

The stuffers return

If I told you that one of today's leading taxidermists is called Stoate, you might think I was pulling your leg; but your scepticism would be misplaced, for Chris Stoate has indeed helped pioneer the revival of a curious art and, although still only twenty-seven, is such an authority that he has brought out a book on it.*

His message is that, after a period in the doldrums, taxidermy is once more a growth industry, and that in the past ten years the craftsmen known uncompromisingly by the Victorians as 'the stuffers' have made a strong comeback. Today between sixty and eighty members of the Guild of Taxidermists will foregather at the British Museum's workshops in the Edgware Road for a seminar which will include talks, demonstrations and an exhibition of work.

In Victorian days stuffed animals, birds and fish were immensely popular: ladies wore hats festooned with parrot wings and owl heads, and gentlemen had the hooves of their favourite horses turned into matchbox holders or feet for chairs. One might imagine that the market for preserved creatures had now died a natural death. Far from it: demand is strong, both from museums which want to renew their exhibits and from private customers who assemble their own collections of sporting or other trophies. The expense is by no means negligible, for even a medium-sized bird such as a magpie or jackdaw costs about £50.

One reason for the revival is that modern techniques developed in America have enabled craftsmen to produce far more lifelike and durable specimens than could be achieved a hundred years ago. Today's taxidermist is not so much a stuffer as a sculptor, who minutely measures the creature he is working on, skins it, models its every bone and muscle in plasticine, takes a mould of the model in fibreglass, and fills the mould with polyurethane foam, which expands and hardens to form a perfect replica of the original body. This

* *Taxidermy: The Revival of a Natural Art* by Christopher Stoate (The Sportsman's Press).

'manikin' is not only light, rigid and immune to decay: it will also receive pins for fixing back the tanned skin of the creature being mounted.

Much of Mr Stoate's book is instructional ('Two alternative incisions for skinning heads of ducks and woodpeckers', and so on). But he also gives an outline of the subject's history and hints at the tensions which today spark between practitioners who work in leisurely fashion for museums and commercial taxidermists, who sometimes palm off unwary customers with rushed and shoddy work. Apparently the trade is infested with rogues and amateurs.

Neither of those terms applies to Mike Windham-Wright, who is widely regarded as one of the most professional of modern commercial taxidermists, and has his workshop south of Oban in Scotland. Big animals are his speciality: he will tackle anything from an elephant to a roe deer – and indeed did mount three elephants during his time in Africa.

He now works largely for customers with sporting interests, and at the moment is about to send off a 22-point red deer stag shot by a Spanish business executive in Scotland to the man's private museum in Spain – a commission worth £3,000. If possible, he likes to be in at the kill himself, so that he can start taking measurements immediately; and for one of his most celebrated *tableaux* – two red deer stags fighting, now in a museum in Glasgow – he shot both the beasts himself.

To someone like him who works with big animals, modern materials bring the advantage of being extremely light. 'One of the elephants I did in Africa weighed seven tons when it was alive,' he recalls. 'But when we'd finished mounting it, eight of us could lift it with no bother.'

Such is the interest in his craft that he is besieged by people wanting to learn and, although he has three students in his workshop, he is forced to turn dozens away. Unemployment being what it is, this seems a pity; but if you should suddenly find that you need an elephant stuffed or mounted (neither term seems entirely free from indelicate associations), at least you know where to apply.

Beat hell out of a bath

The pleasure of demolishing a cast-iron bath with a 3-lb hammer is not one that can be indulged in every day, and I daresay it would pall if repeated too often. But a good smash-up every now and then does wonders for morale.

The bath which I had occasion to batter was an ancient, upright model which some former owner of the farm had used as a cattle trough. Chipped and rusty though it was, with its plughole blocked by a lump of concrete, it did the job well enough; but since it was no beauty and we had enough proper troughs anyway, I decided to get rid of it. Only then did I discover what a prodigious weight it was. Sixty years ago – or whenever it came into being – baths were baths and none of your flimsy plastic. This monster weighed several hundredweight, and the only way to load it into a trailer was to break it up first.

Having always believed that cast-iron is brittle, I was amazed to find my first few hammer blows bouncing off. Something about the curvature of the bath's sides and bottom seemed to give it tensile strength, and only after a prolonged assault did cracks begin to appear. Then at last a chunk flew out, and with a triumphant hail of blows I had the whole thing in half. The rest was easy. Its overall resistance gone, the tub collapsed into a heap of easily handled pieces, and these are now reposing at the bottom of a pit in the wood, where in years to come they may perhaps puzzle some latterday archaeologist.

Yet the banishing of the bath, though welcome on every count, also taught me a general truth about the removal of eyesores. For months I wanted it away, and now I am delighted to be shot of it: the field looks much better without it. Yet my satisfaction is not something that can be shared with visitors. It is no use saying, 'There used to be a filthy old bath there, in the corner.' To a newcomer, the statement conveys practically nothing. To go on about it is to risk classification with the tourist who, returning from Kenya and boring friends rigid with photographs of the bush, says, 'Such a pity – there *was* a lion just to the left of that thorn tree, but somehow I missed it.' All right, there was a lion. There was also a bath; but now that it is gone and I have had the fun of smashing it, I shall not mention it again.

MAY

Great burst of garlic

Suddenly it is wild garlic time again. In the great bomb-burst of leaves and flowers brought on by the hot weather, nothing has been more extraordinary than the speed with which the garlic, known locally as ramsons, has sprung from the dead-looking forest floor into a carpet eight or ten inches deep. Already the first of the starlike white flowers are beginning to come out. The sight, however, is nothing to the smell, which can only be described as prodigious. Not merely in the woods themselves, but also, if the air-currents are right, in the fields below, one is knocked sideways by clouds of the most pungent scent. Old-timers say that in pre-myxomatosis days a rabbit hunted by dogs through the garlic came out so highly spiced that it could go straight into the pot without further seasoning – and from the way my boots stink when I come in from a walk, I can well believe it.

Writ in weed-killer

The lawns of Oxford colleges look particularly luscious at this time of year. Great sweeps of immaculate emerald velvet, flawlessly striped, they excite in me both straight admiration and pangs of jealousy. Why does my own patch of moss, daisies, dandelions and buttercups fall so far short of these perfect swards?

The answer is simply that I do not spend enough time and money on it. I remember once overhearing our college head gardener explain his secret to an inquiring American tourist. 'All you have to do,' he said, 'is mow it and roll it and spike it and fertilize it and kill the weeds, and mow it and roll it, and go on doing that for 300 years – and then you should have a reasonable lawn.'

Alas, not all the undergraduates of my day shared the visitor's reverence for horticulture. After a particularly riotous dinner members of the rowing club took it into their heads to inscribe their towpath war-cry – 'Ollie Ollie, Wuggins!' – on the lawn in the middle of the front quad, and late at night they burned the letters into the sacred turf by pouring out trails of household detergent powder, which acts as a powerful herbicide.

The mortification of the head gardener can be imagined. The young gentlemen were heavily fined and paid for the ruined turf to be replaced, but it was several years before the last traces of their vandalism grew out. Meanwhile another faction, including myself, was galvanized into action by the approach of a fête to be held by the university Conservative Association on the lawn of Blenheim Palace, a few miles out to the west.

Somehow we conceived it our bounden duty to write VOTE LABOUR on the Duke of Marlborough's lawn. Midnight thus found us scaling his high park wall on the outskirts of Woodstock, with our commando jackets belted in at the waist to form capacious pouches, which we had loaded with packets of Daz. The night was very dark, and progress through the trees difficult; but after a circuitous approach we arrived on the lawn in front of the palace just as the tower clock struck 1 am with a melancholy tenor chime. Then, at the critical moment, our spirits quailed.

The expanse of grass was so vast and flat that we felt we could not wreck it. To have done so would have been to offer personal insult and injury to the Duke, against whom we had no grudge at all. So we withdrew to the bank of Capability Brown's lake and did our mischief there, writing out the slogan on the rough, sloping turf in the hope that it would take the eye of everyone driving in to the show.

In the event we were foiled by the length of the grass. On a close-shaven surface the washing powder had produced a reaction overnight; but here several days went by before any difference became noticeable, and the fête passed off without anyone realizing that an outrage had been perpetrated. Only after the mob had come and gone did our message appear – to the considerable mystification of ordinary visitors.

To the toads' rescue

I cannot claim to be an ardent fancier of toads. Somehow the creatures, warts and all, do not strike me as very appealing. All the same, I am delighted to hear that England's first ever toad tunnel is proving a triumphant success.

Until this year several thousand toads were killed every spring on the road between Henley-on-Thames and Marlow, as they headed down out of the lovely hill country round Hambleden towards their spawning grounds beside the Thames. In spite of the devoted efforts of local helpers, who did their best to marshal the migrants and carry them across the death-strip by the bucketful, the massacre was such that at times the road became dangerous to humans as well, as it was carpeted with a greasy mass of squashed corpses.

This year, however, things have been entirely different, thanks to a tunnel installed as a joint project by the Fauna and Flora Preservation Society and a firm called ACO Polymer. In fact there are two tunnels, but so far only one has been opened; it is nearly twenty yards long with fences of twelve-inch-high polythene funnelling in to the entrance, and so well does it suit the migrants that already at least 3,000 have hopped through. (The passers-by have been counted by a photo-electric cell; but, since a good many are in pairs, already joined together and copulating as they go, each blip has been reckoned to indicate a toad and a half.)

The organizers are delighted and reckon that mortality has been cut by ninety per cent. On the peak evening 570 toads went through, and about 1,000 more were moving in along the approach fences,

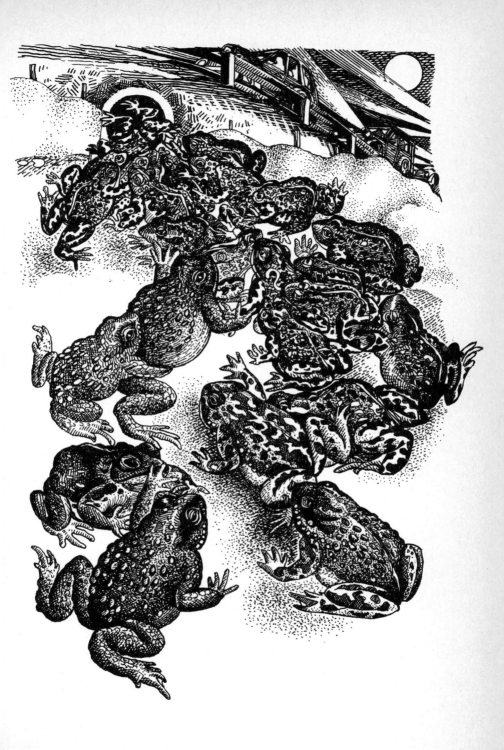

some after journeys of up to four miles. Yet, even with the mating urge upon them, the creatures are remarkably sensitive to mechanical noise or vibration and seem to have learned that it pays to wait until after the pub exodus at 11 pm before they set out. Rush-hour in the tunnel lasts from 1 am to 3 am.

It is clear that much of the success is due to the shape of the conduit itself. Known to the manufacturers as Q 200, tunnels of this kind were originally designed as drains and are made of polymer concrete, which contains a plastic resin and so does not flake or become dusty. Along the upper surface they have ventilation slits, which admit both light and moisture, thus helping to create conditions which toads find amenable.

In matters of toad welfare we are way behind the West Germans, who opened their first tunnel in 1979. But now that the Marlow experiment has proved such a life-saver, there are hopes that it can be repeated in dozens more of the 250 major migration sites recorded in Britain.

It seems sad to reflect that almost all the extra toads preserved by the tunnel will in the end be eaten by one of the species that prey on them – owls, buzzards, foxes, badgers, hedgehogs and grass snakes among them. But I suppose that if you are *Bufo bufo* it is better at least to have a chance of survival, and to form part of a food-chain designed by evolution, than to be senselessly obliterated by a mechanical monster screaming over tarmac.

Defeated by smells

To move through the woods these days is to be bombarded from every direction. From above comes an intermittent hail of papery husks cast off by opening beech leaves. From all sides come volleys of insects. Yet, even more than the physical objects, it is the smells that assault the walker. A short while ago I mentioned the wild garlic, now at its peak. Whole hillsides are awash with scent: it is as if a thousand Italian chefs had run amok in an open-air contest to produce the strongest possible spaghetti *aglio e olio*. But turn in the other direction and you are hit by a scarcely less stupefying blast of bluebells.

If the smells are so powerful to humans, what are they like to dogs?

I keep thinking of an experiment in which, by progressively reducing the traces of a particular scent below the level at which it could be detected by humans, researchers showed that a dog's sense of smell is some 700 times as acute as that of a person.

I can only conclude that dogs have some kind of automatic filter mechanism which shuts out smells of no interest to them. If, on our walks, my Labradors were inhaling literally 700 times what I am inhaling, they would surely self-destruct; as it is, they can somehow cut out the garlic and continue to work the line of the old cock pheasant which ran through it into the grass.

One in the eye from a bee

The acquisition of two more beehives – one occupied, one empty – should greatly have strengthened our domestic economy; but the importation of some 10,000 new workers and their accommodation was not accomplished without certain setbacks.

The journey home went smoothly, as did the setting up of the inhabited hive, which contained a young swarm of docile, yellowish New Zealand bees. Trouble set in when I began to fit the empty one – a handsome blue-and-white model known as a WBC – as an outer shell round an old hive tenanted by a swarm of much darker, almost black bees well known to be bad tempered.

I waited till dusk, plugged the entrance with foam rubber and set about my carpentry, but the job proved trickier than expected and full dark had fallen before it was complete. From the evil whine which emanated, I could tell that the inmates were not amused, but they had no means of escape. Eventually I unplugged the doorway by pulling out the foam rubber with a string and came away.

Next morning, observing from a safe distance, I decided that the bees had settled down well and were working normally. Most of them were. But one had evidently not forgotten the indignity of being thumped and jolted around the night before. I was kneeling down, screwing a hinge to the orchard gatepost, when something made me glance up. A single bee was coming like a bullet for my face. There could be no doubt that the attack was deliberate – a low-level, under-the-radar sortie direct from hive to target. I just had time to shut my eyes, when bingo!

Luckily no lasting damage was done. But the sting and part of the bee's abdomen had to be exhumed from my upper eyelid, and for two days that eye was almost closed by a horrible, dropsical swelling. Now more than ever I endorse the verdict of the local apiarist who exclaimed with feeling, 'It be the black buggers do for I.'

Flight of the peregrine

Four hundred feet below, deep between hanging oak woods and vertical cliffs of limestone, the Wye winds like a brown satin ribbon through the coils of the gorge. But up here on the wonderful vantage-point of Symond's Yat Rock, half way to the sky, even an earth-bound human almost feels that he can fly. Both ecologically and aesthetically, the high, wild surroundings exactly suit the birds that everyone has come to see: the peregrine.

For the sixth year running the same pair of peregrines is nesting in a hole that runs back four or five feet into the sheer face of one of the cliffs. Until Monday it was thought that they had two chicks, but now it is established that they have three. Both the tiercel (male) and falcon (female) are easily recognizable – he by the bright yellow round his beak and on his legs, she by a white patch on her left wing; and on this splendid rock, poised in mid-air some 500 yards from the nest, there is nothing but space between you and them.

Three powerful telescopes set up on the wall of the observation point give an admirable view. There sits the falcon, brooding her three chicks, with her dark head turning constantly to right and left as she gazes out. Occasionally a little ball of white fluff becomes visible beneath or to one side of her. Her vigilance never relaxes – and the phenomenal power of her eyesight was confirmed by an incident the other day. Her mate, out hunting over the hills to the north, killed a pigeon. He was so far away that human watchers with binoculars could hardly see him, but *she* saw him and instantly came streaking out to take the kill in a 'food pass', snatching the prey from his talons to hers high over the gorge.

This is one of the great joys of the Symond's Yat site – that much of the peregrines' activity takes place in full view. So close do the hawks come to the observation point and so fast do they pass by that you can sometimes hear the rippling rush of their feathers cutting the air.

Fortunate visitors witness that most thrilling of all aerial manoeuvres, the stop, in which the peregrine dives on pigeon or dove or jackdaw like a bullet, with wings folded almost shut, at speeds up to 120 miles per hour, and grabs it in full flight. It is for this phenomenal feat that evolution has set the hawks' eyes at the most streamlined angle possible and furnished them with baffles in their nostrils which break up the wind at extreme velocity.

Sometimes when an aerial chase develops, with both hawks hunting together, one high, one low, spectators become so caught up in the pursuit that they shout out with excitement and start calling the turns – 'He's going left, he's climbing, he's dived. . .'. So popular has the site become that last year it attracted some 70,000 people.

Yet for most of the time one needs to be patient. On the afternoon I was there, the falcon sat brooding for hours on end, and even when a white domestic duck made a provocative – not to say suicidal – fly-past, up the river and right across the face of the cliff below the nest, she did not stir. But then her mate launched out from the cliff on a sortie and the sight of him flickering away like a slate-grey arrowhead into the hills was enough to set adrenalin racing. Was any bird of prey ever more beautiful or deadly?

This traditional site for an eyrie was abandoned during the 1950s, when numbers of peregrines were drastically reduced by the long-term effects of organochlorine pesticides; but it was reoccupied in 1982, when three young were reared, and has been used ever since. Now, during the breeding season, it is looked after jointly by the Forestry Commission and the Royal Society for the Protection of Birds.

This year, as soon as it was known that the falcon had laid, RSPB climbers went down over the cliff-top one evening to mark the four eggs. In the daytime two or more wardens are on duty, and the nest is under continuous surveillance; at night, the caravan in which the wardens sleep is wired up to alarm systems which sound off if any intruder attempts to approach the site. Even if someone did manage to steal an egg or a chick, the chances are that he would not get far, for with the help of the local police an effective system has been devised for sealing off the entire area.

The same is not true elsewhere, for the RSPB cannot protect all the peregrines breeding in Britain (now estimated to number about 1,000 pairs), and in 1986 some fifty sites were robbed. With a female chick worth up to £1,000 on the black market and a male about £750, the incentive is strong and demand is insatiable, especially from the Middle East.

In a typical incident at this time last year a German falconer called Rudi Pfabe was apprehended in Hull as he sought to board a ferry for home. In his car, incubating on a hot-water bottle, were three peregrine eggs which he had got from a contact in the Yorkshire Dales. He and the Englishman were each fined £600.

The success of the Symond's Yat eyrie seems to augur well for Birdwatch Europe '87, billed by the RSPB as the biggest mass observation ever organized. Due to run for the whole of next week, the event has been launched with a grant of £70,000 from the European Community and aims to stimulate interest in birds throughout the continent.

A cynic might protest that no such stimulus is needed in Britain, for the RSPB already has 450,000 members and an income of £7 million, and is by far the largest organization of its kind in the world. Yet there is definitely a need for propaganda in less civilized places such as Italy and Spain, where small songbirds are shot and caught by the million, and in Malta, where, it is estimated, some 30,000 swallows are shot every year purely for target practice.

If the last such exercise is anything to go by, next week's turn-out will be immense. Birdwatch UK, held on a cold winter's day in January 1986, fetched out more than 25,000 people to 150 sites. This time 250 sites will be open in Britain alone – and altogether twelve nations are taking part.

What the birds will make of it is another matter. Their descendants may well benefit in the long run, but in the short term the mass turn-out of fanciers may prove rather tiresome. Personally, if I were a bird, I should take steps to make myself scarce from Monday to Saturday – or, if I were continually airborne, like a swift, I should put myself into a higher orbit for the duration.

Fêtes worse than death

Once again we are fast approaching the season of that dreaded institution, the village fête. To people who drop in for a casual tour of cricket field or rectory garden and go away with the comfortable feeling that they have helped some worthy local cause by spending a pound or two the occasion no doubt seems easy and enjoyable, especially if the afternoon is fine; but those landed with the burden of organizing the show derive no more than moderate amusement from referring to it as a fête worse than death.

The arguments and tensions which it generates are amazing, not least because one or more of the vital *dramatis personae* is always in a sulk, offended by some insult which, since it was probably imagined in the first place, is not easily soothed away. If the maestro of the goldfish stand or the wizard of the white elephant stall cannot be persuaded to perform, the sky will fall.

Disputes are perennial: settled one year, the same controversies flare up again acrimoniously the next. Should the committee go to the trouble and expense of getting some locally based actor or other celebrity to open the fête? And, if we do, why can we not have an embargo on the sale of produce before the official opening? Unless forcibly restrained, locals sweep down on the home-made cakes and jam like vultures, so that by the time the big-wig comes past, declaring the show open, the tables have already been reduced to an embarrassing jumble and only a few part-worn tarts remain.

It is these stalls that make the big money. Sideshows like the coconut shy, bowling, darts, crockery smashing, penny rolling and bran-tubs are essential, for they give customers something to *do*, but it is the sales of food, vegetables, plants and teas that really bring in the cash, along with Chinese raffles for bottles and the inevitable tombola.

I am a dab hand – though I must not boast – at running Trap the Rat, in which a ratlike dummy is slid down a tilted drainpipe and the customer tries to swat it with a stick as it emerges. But my speciality is Have a Bash, which requires clients to hammer six-inch nails into a baulk of timber.

'Fewest hits wins', says the sign. '10p per nail'. It is not as easy as it looks, for the wood is the hardest, knottiest old bit of dead elm that I have been able to dredge up and the hammer is a miserable specimen with a slippery metal grip. Hefty young louts, having criticized the weapon and delivered themselves of a few oaths, lash out like madmen, missing frequently, and by the fifteenth or twentieth stroke have flattened the nail sideways beyond hope of redemption. The prize is invariably won by one of the farm hands, foresters or fencing contractors who wield a hammer as part of their job; after a cool appraisal, they hit hard and straight with a slow rhythm, and to the incredulity of the louts get the nail fully home with only five or six blows.

One year, for a change, I rigged up a kind of aerial railway, down which boys could hurtle on a little round seat suspended from a monkey wheel. The upper end of the rope was secured to the top branches of a birch tree on the common, the bottom to the roof of a Land Rover parked on the cricket field below. I spent the whole afternoon up the tree, responding with vigorous gestures to the occasional cries of 'Like a banana?' and launching young customers (who came up by ladder) down the line.

All went well until the arrival of our local MP, whom I had better not identify except by saying that he had a lot of blond, floppy hair. When he announced that he wanted a go, I told him he was much too heavy, that the contraption was meant for boys only, that the nylon rope would stretch, and that he would land on his backside in the gorse at the edge of the field.

Undeterred, up he came and, having made sure that a photographer from the local newspaper was in position, he launched off. Sure enough, he came to rest in the gorse bush, but not before the shutter had clicked – and there he was in next week's paper, flying through the air, Tarzan to the life.

Perhaps my greatest coup came a year later, when, besides my other responsibilities, I was in charge of the tug-of-war team. There was no escape, for the event was prominently billed on the programme as the Sun Inn versus the Woodman, to take place in the central arena at 4.30.

At about 4.15 I began to round up my team. Soon I had dug out all except one – but of Brian, landlord of the Sun and my anchorman, there was no sign. By 4.25 I was getting desperate. Ignominy was threatening. Then I had a brainwave: the man who had brought the Bouncy Castle. He was colossal – a meat-mountain on his own. Pavarotti, put beside him, would have looked a shrimp. He must have weighed twenty-five stone. I hurried to his corner of the ground and, observing that he had no bouncers at that moment, went up to him.

'You got a minute?' I asked.

'I might have. Why?'

'Step this way.'

At the sight of him, in a straining yellow T-shirt, the Woodman lads fell about and declared themselves buggered. Nor were they far wrong. By the time he had wrapped one end of the rope round his waist, there was only just enough left for the other seven of our team to latch on to; but, when the referee called out, 'Take the strain . . . Are you ready? . . . *Pull!*' he simply leaned backwards, and the entire Woodman team came flat on its face. When we changed ends for the second round, the same thing happened and we won the best of three effortlessly.

And Brian? It later transpired that four pints of Wadworth XXXXX, taken at incautious speed in the beer tent, had painlessly erased all memory of the tug-of-war and that he had gone to sleep behind some shrubs. When he awoke and found that dark had fallen, he sensibly went home. He was no mean weight – sixteen stone, I should guess – but even so he would have been worth not much more than half the outsize anchor-man with whom fate, at the last moment, had furnished us.

Up the bull-removal squad!

Connoisseurs of the ridiculous have been disappointed to find that the Labour general election manifesto contains scarcely any of the grandiose proposals for reform in the countryside put forward at the Party's conference last September. In particular, I mourn the disappearance of the promise that 'threats to the enjoyment of the countryside . . . such as bulls in fields crossed by public rights of way will be removed.'

It was the word 'removed' that appealed so strongly; and for me – as, I imagine, for countless other fans – there were only two possible candidates for the post of Director of the Bull-Removal Squad: Messrs Healey and Hattersley. I can easily imagine either cruising into action dressed in Wild West gear, whirling lassos and giving crisp, definitive orders into walkie-talkie radios.

But to descend from farce to reality: in my experience, if you do have trouble with a bull, there is usually no time to call for help or appeal to the authorities, no matter how powerful they may be. I shall never forget the winter evening when, after a fruitless attempt to flight pigeons in a small beech wood, I decided to go home and vaulted the fence into a field. Scarcely had I landed when I heard a thunder of hooves to my right and turned to see an immense Hereford bull in the final stages of a charge. There was no chance of evasive action. A second later I was lifted clean off the ground and hurled into the barbed wire on my left, with the animal hammering me from the right.

Thank heavens, it was polled – for if it had had horns, I do not think I would have survived. Even so, I was in severe trouble from the violence of its onslaught. Oddly enough, although taking punishment heavily, I somehow had time to reflect that here was a perfect illustration of the phrase 'brute force'. Seen from above, the neck of the bovine battering ram was eighteen inches wide, and when I punched it as hard as I could, I made as much impression as I would have on granite. It also occurred to me that if only I could reason with it and say, 'Look here, old chap, I'm sure we can sort this out amicably,' things would have been easier.

The bull, however, was in no mood for conversation – and what happened next, I have never been quite sure, for I was knocked out in the process. When I came to, I was back in the wood, lying on the ground, with a square foot torn from the seat of my trousers flapping from the top strand of the fence. I presume I must have tried to make a dash for the safety of the trees and got caught on the way. In any event, my valuable shotgun was lying on the ground between the bull's front feet, some three yards out of reach. Having made sure that all my limbs were functioning, I managed to recover the weapon by fishing it back with a long stick; and – so shaken and angry was I by then – I let drive with both barrels right over the top of his head, as close to his skull as I dared aim.

The broadside had no effect whatever, unless to increase the fury with which he was scraping the ground and rolling his bloodshot eyes. I therefore withdrew and limped back to my Land Rover by a circuitous route. At home I discovered that I was black and blue all down my right-hand side and well ripped up on the left.

But what did I do? Did I lobby my local MP for the instant creation of a new Ministry of Environmental Protection and a Wildlife and Countryside Enforcement Agency and a Bull-Removal Squad? Of course not. I had a hot bath and a large whisky, disinfected my wounds and told myself not to be such a bloody fool next time.

Vermin control needed

Half the shell of a pheasant's egg lying on the woodland path betrayed the work of a crow, magpie or jay. In our immediate environs, where there is no game preservation, such predators abound – with the result that there are scarcely any wild game-birds and far fewer birds of all descriptions than there would be if some measure of control were exercised over the more destructive species.

The effect of reducing the carrion crow population has been demonstrated again and again, but nowhere more strikingly than in Eskdalemuir, the huge new forest in Dumfriesshire. Before trees were planted there twenty-five years ago, scarcely forty species of birds scratched a living from the bare hills. Now, in the 35,000 acres of woodland, there are nearly 120 – partly because the trees have given them shelter, but largely because wildlife officers cull more than 1,000 crows and over 100 mink every year.

One can argue for days about how far it is right or desirable for humans to manage wild creatures, but surely it is sensible to keep down those with really destructive habits – and anyone who claims that crows are innocuous might like to consider the following story, told me recently by a Welsh hill-farmer.

One of his ewes, weakened by lambing, rolled over on the mountainside, became wedged on her back against a clump of rushes and could not regain her feet. By the time he found her next morning, the whole of her udder had been eaten away by crows. She was still alive and survived, but obviously could never rear another lamb – and the ordeal she had been through scarcely bears thinking about.

Another pest rampant at this time of year is the grey squirrel. Between now and July squirrels will do millions of pounds' worth of damage by gnawing away the bark of young hardwood trees, mainly on or just above the roots. Many of the trees will die and a great many more will be permanently stunted.

Why squirrels do this, scientists are still not sure, even after years of research. Some people believe that the reasons are nutritional, and that the attacks start when the sap is rising at its fastest and the bark at its most delicious. But, according to another theory, the whole process is dictated by territorial imperatives and young male squirrels are marking out their ground. Either way, it amounts to silvicultural disaster – and the answer, as with crows, is surely control of the population, carried out as humanely as possible.

Tale of two barn owls

How do you sex a barn owl? Only with difficulty is the answer. Females are generally larger and tend to have more brown spots on their breasts, but even if you have a bird in your hand you cannot be certain whether it is male or female unless you resort to the extreme expedient of surgery.

This truth has just been brought home to some neighbours, who offered a home to a pair of captive owls to see if they would rear a family which could be released to supplement the dwindling wild population. The birds came from the Slimbridge Wildfowl Trust on the banks of the Severn, where the conservation officer, David Paynter, has been running an owl unit and has released twenty-two birds into the wild over the past three years.

It was last November when he installed this particular pair in their foster-home – a spacious loft, wired off to prevent escape, in a stone barn on top of the Cotswold escarpment. Since then their human host and hostess have kept them supplied with a daily ration of dead day-old chicks (bought deep-frozen for £3 a hundred) supplemented by the odd rat for variety.

On this diet the owls seemed to thrive, spending daylight hours in their box near the rafters and emerging at dusk to fly about the barn. Certainly they were most handsome birds, with snow-white faces and beautiful plumage overall; and, although they both looked much the same, one had a habit of standing bolt upright at the back of the box if any human approached closely during the day, whereas the other slid down into a curious sitting position – a difference which nurtured hopes that they were husband and wife.

April, however, brought disappointment, for no eggs appeared, and the lady of the house began to tease her husband by saying that his owls were queer, and that he had obviously been palmed off with two old gays. Even so, it was the end of May before the humans discovered that two other owls still at Slimbridge – also allegedly a pair – had laid eight eggs between them.

Although barn owls are prolific and often produce between six and nine round, white eggs each, the sheer speed of production prompted another examination. This strongly suggested that the two by the Severn were females and the two in the hills male. So now an exchange has been effected – in time, everyone hopes, for both pairs to start again and breed.

Everyone who likes owls must wish them well, for a survey carried out between 1982 and 1985 by the Hawk Trust (an independent charity) shows that the number of barn owls in England, Scotland and Wales has declined by about half since the last census, carried out in 1932, to the present level of some 6,000 pairs. The main cause has been the disappearance of rough grassland, which forms the owls' favourite habitat, and the consequent drop in their main prey species, voles.

Another lethal influence has been the increase in fast motor traffic, particularly on motorways, where barn owls tend to hunt the rough grass verges with their characteristic method of coasting low over the ground. The Hawk Trust's report, published in 1987, puts road casualties at 6,000 a year or one bird from every family, and suggests that mortality in the first year of life is about seventy per cent.

To help augment the wild population the Trust maintains a large aviary containing over fifty owls in Buckinghamshire. Many of these birds are survivors of road accidents or offspring of earlier casualties which have recovered and been brought in by well-wishers from as far afield as Skye and the tip of Cornwall, and their young are released into the wild.

Yet even with this artificial topping up, experts are not optimistic about raising numbers in general. The trouble is that barn owls are sedentary birds and do not usually range more than a kilometre or so from the building which they inhabit; now that the population has sunk so low, there has been a widespread loss of continuity, with one occupied site too far from the next for contact to be maintained. This means that, if a single pair is released, its offspring are unlikely to breed, and the Trust's aim is to 'bomb' areas of good habitat with thirty or forty pairs at a time. But is it not the saddest of pictures: a solitary white owl moping out its life alone for want of a mate within call?

Aloft for the sunset

Where better to spend the last hour of daylight than high in the branches of an ancient oak? Some people may deem it childish to derive pleasure from climbing trees; I like to feel that the satisfaction is deeply atavistic, springing from the far-off days when our ancestors spent much of their time aloft.

In any event, I relax in this fork some fifty feet above the ground and reflect on the tree's great age. It was certainly growing strong when Queen Victoria came to the throne; quite possibly it already stood there in the hedgerow when civil war swept the land in 1642.

You are close to history, then, as you perch on its mighty limbs and feel the roughness of its bark. But the main point of it, for me, is that it makes an ideal observation platform. Animals do not look upwards much and our telltale smell is carried off above their heads, so that from our vantage-point we should be able to watch, unseen and unscented, anything that comes out in the dusk on to the grass field between us and the wood.

We are facing west, into a blaze of sunset: but here comes a storm, riding in on the breeze. Black clouds blot out the sun. Light dims rapidly, colours fade. Perhaps our oak was already here when Milton wrote:

Now came still evening on, and twilight gray
Had in her sober livery all things clad.

In 300 years nothing has changed: leaves, trunks, grass, hedgerow – all turn monochrome. But look: on the edge of the wood a slender

white shape has materialized. Binoculars reveal it as a fallow doe, graceful and slim. She stands facing us, looking out over the field. Behind her something darker moves restlessly up and down. Her fawn is eager to start grazing, but she, with the caution of maturity, blocks its way until she feels secure. Then she tucks up her front legs and sails easily over the fence into the field.

Rain begins to patter on the leaves. With a whoosh of wings a pigeon arrives to perch just above us. So long as we keep still, it does not see us, but sidles up and down the branches, selecting a comfortable roost.

Something makes me look down: almost directly beneath us is a fox, deep red-brown in the twilight, moving out on its night patrol. From over to our left the twang of fence-wire betrays the arrival of more deer in the field: my glasses reveal four more dark shapes already grazing.

The rain stops. The storm has passed, but night is falling and the light has almost gone. Owls are tuning up in the valley. A party of mallard goes past unseen, snickering out its urgent in-flight messages. Even through binoculars the deer are almost invisible, ghostly dun lumps that blur into the background.

Now, climb down without a sound and creep silently away, for to disturb a scene so peaceful would be an act of desecration.

In the cherry orchard

English cherries, held back by the cold, wet weather, will not be ripe for another week or so, but scare guns are already blasting off in orchards to the chagrin of anyone living within earshot, and local flocks of starlings spend most of the daylight hours in orbit, constantly accelerated by the unceasing detonations.

The cherry harvest never comes round without my thinking fondly of Old Jack, a farmer whose memories reach back to the early years of the century. As a boy he used to earn a penny a day as a human scarecrow, patrolling an orchard and every now and then discharging an ancient muzzle-loader. At lunchtime he got an hour off, but, to make sure that the enemy had no respite, his place was always taken by a friend.

One day as usual he handed over the weapon and went off for his dinner. The other boy, mistakenly thinking that the gun had recently been fired, rammed a second charge of black powder down the barrel on top of the first – and, when he next pulled the trigger, standing in front of a wooden stable, gave himself a nasty surprise.

'What happened, Jack? What happened?' we ask – for although we have heard the story many times before, we always long for a repetition of the punchline.

'Oh!' comes the unfailing answer. 'It put him through the boards.'

I carry in my head an indelible picture of Jack's comrade-in-arms – flat on his back, eyes smarting, head ringing, hair on end, collar-bone numb – gazing with incredulity at his own silhouette punched in the flimsy boards of the stable wall.

Today, as far as I know, no fruit-growers fire muzzle-loaders to protect their crops; but birds are as great a nuisance as ever, and starlings a menace second to none – for whereas other species such as blackbirds pick single cherries and eat them on the ground in civilized fashion, a starling pecks frenziedly at every red blob within reach, thereby creating havoc. Worst of all are fledgling birds, which lay about themselves with the abandon of teenage hooligans.

To keep them at bay, a variety of scarers is used. The simplest are the ropes of bangers which smoulder away – faster in the wind – and go off with a flash, a report and a puff of smoke every twenty minutes or so. Heavier explosions are produced by propane gas guns. These can be adjusted to detonate at any chosen interval, but their very regularity is a disadvantage, for birds become accustomed to their rhythm and learn to dodge in for a quick snack between reports. More sophisticated models governed by microchips, which can vary the bowling and produce double detonations, are now coming in, but they cost £400 or £500 apiece.

Happily boys are not entirely superseded, even if posterity has armed them with different weapons. At Grove Farms near Harwell, in Oxfordshire, for instance – one of the largest cherry orchards in the country – two or three students are put up in a caravan for the five-week season and paid to ride around from 5 am until dusk on mopeds from which the silencers have been removed.

'I've found it isn't much use patrolling on foot,' says the general manager, Chris Manuel. 'The starlings just fly off ahead of you and come in behind you. But a moped's too fast for them. It arrives too suddenly, and they don't like that.'

The cost of maintaining such rip-roaring patrols is by no means negligible. Nor is the noise. With cannons booming, bangers popping and bikes howling for fifteen hours a day – to say nothing of birds screeching from a mixture of alarm and frustration – the cacophony is appalling. But with the orchard producing an annual crop of between 90 and 100 tons of cherries, the stakes are high, and for five weeks no holds are barred.

Uninvited guest

Meet Pidge, our resident pigeon, who arrived uninvited during the winter and is now *de facto* a member of the establishment. Since he wears no ring or tag, it is impossible to say where he came from, but he is clearly not of local origin. His colouring – dark, slatey blue, with a bold white patch on the back – suggests that he is every inch a Londoner. If he is, he has come a long way.

Were his manner less assured, I might be afraid that he was suffering an identity crisis, for at some times he seems to think he is a chicken and at others he behaves like a peacock. He consorts with all the farmyard birds on terms of absolute familiarity, strutting among them, sharing their food and copying their mannerisms as if he were one of their kind. Yokels like wild wood pigeons and collared doves do not amuse him: he drives them off with the utmost arrogance. Whenever he overreaches himelf and provokes a riposte from peacock or cockerel, he relies on his vertical take-off capability to get himself out of trouble.

Once, early in the spring, we thought he had fallen victim to Pussy, our neighbour's cat. Morning disclosed a large patch of feathers – clearly his – by the gate of the vegetable garden, and we feared the worst, especially when he did not appear for several days. But then he bobbed up again, looking a bit patchy, and we could see that he had had a near miss.

I call Pidge 'he' as though I know he is a gentleman. But he may equally well be a lady – and indeed over the past few weeks he has shown signs of going broody, scratching nests out of the dust on ledges in the barn and uttering particularly suggestive crooning noises, thick and low. But as he has certainly not laid eggs and has no mate about, I am beginning to think it is all a front, put on to defuse potentially embarrassing questions.

Occasionally, as a flock of racing pigeons goes whistling overhead,

I fancy I see a nostalgic look creep into his little orange eyes. Yet the truth is that he has grown stout with easy living and his rotundity is now so marked that I do not think he could keep up with such high-fliers even if he wanted to.

Great north-south divide

The south is rich, the north poor; and the problem of how to reverse the drift of money, jobs and people is clearly one of the most intractable facing the Government. Yet Mrs Thatcher may perhaps take comfort from reflecting on the way in which the pendulum has swung in the past.

At the beginning of the nineteenth century the valley in which we live, in the south-west, was one of the most prosperous in England. Eighteen woollen mills, powered by the stream, turned out cloth of such high quality that demand for it was strong all over the world, not least in Russia. The mill-owners made fortunes and built themselves elegant stone houses; one man, said to have started with only £50, made a net income in a single year of £24,000, with which he paid the architect George Repton to build him a handsome country home on the ridge looking out over the Severn towards Wales. Even the workers did exceptionally well, earning up to two guineas a week or nearly five times the highest rate that a farm hand could hope for. The population grew rapidly to more than 2,000.

Then everything began to change. In 1810 mills in Yorkshire started to produce fine cloth more cheaply than the south could manage, partly because they had invented a new process, partly because they were powered by coal. Slowly at first, then with gathering speed, the initiative – and the money – passed to the north, and our valley went into a decline.

One after another the mills closed. Because there was no such thing as state unemployment benefit, people left destitute had to be supported by rates levied on local landowners, several of whom were ruined. Many men, in despair, took to drink, leaving their wives to starve. In 1830 the old workhouse was repaired and reopened to take in the three or four most desperate families. When the last of the big mills shut down in 1837 – and the employees found the doors locked when they arrived for work one Monday morning – it must have seemed that the world had come to an end.

The people knew little of the market forces which had killed their thriving industry, and had no means of finding out why they had been so cruelly dispossessed. Small wonder that they began to emigrate, first to Canada, later to Australia. By 1881 the population of the valley had been halved.

Many of the houses fell into disrepair and collapsed. Today the stumps of walls in the corner of a field or patches of snowdrops flourishing incongruously in the middle of a wood are all that remain to show that cottages stood on those sites long ago. Yet new houses have been built, and the wool merchants' mansions still grace the village street. The place is well-to-do again, enjoying the general prosperity of the south, and a casual visitor would never guess that it had plunged from an era of plenty into a period of extreme hardship and then come up once more.

Difficult though it is to imagine the pendulum ever swinging back so violently, only a reckless punter would predict that something similar will not happen again. Suppose gold were discovered in substantial quantities beneath the moors above Bolton (for example), on a large estate whose owner was prepared to give up his grouse and sell concessions to prospectors. Might that not set off a rush to the north of the kind that the Government would give its eye-teeth to provoke?

The car that flew

At first glance it looks like an old farm trailer, abandoned upside down in the middle of the field. Because the young wheat stands knee-high and undamaged all round it, the eye naturally assumes that it has been there for years and that the farmer has been too idle to tow it away. Closer inspection, however, shows that it is a car which has recently come to a nasty end. And how did it get there without blazing a trail through the crop? Answer: it flew.

One tends to associate accidents with main roads and motorways, and the horror of a crash seems bad enough in high-technology surroundings; but when a smash occurs in the depths of the country, the sheer violence of it strikes a still more sickening note. Crumpled steel and shattered glass make a fearful contrast with soft, green, growing corn.

This crash happened at about nine o'clock one evening. The car was travelling at high speed, probably at least ninety miles per hour. On a slight left-hand bend the driver saw a line of other vehicles approaching from the opposite direction and swerved suddenly to pull back on to his side of the road. His near-side front wheel struck the verge, a grass bank about a foot high. The impact was such that the car took off, clipped two courses from the top of a stone wall, ripped away the side of a big elder bush, flew bodily more than thirty yards through the air, bounced on its wheels, took off again, flew another twenty yards, somersaulting as it went, and came to rest on its roof, squashed nearly flat. Miraculously, the driver was not killed. Rescuers found him still conscious, hanging in his seat-belt, apparently unmarked, with his head sticking out through a split that had burst open between the door and the front wing. He is now being treated for severe injuries to his spine.

I am sorry for him, but uneasy also to think that the remains of his vehicle are going to lie where they are, in full view of other drivers, for at least the next six weeks. Obviously the car is a write-off and, because it landed so far from the road and such a distance from a gateway, any attempt to recover it would destroy a great deal of corn. The insurance company has therefore agreed to leave it until after the harvest, which cannot come before the beginning of August, at the earliest. So for perhaps two months the wreck will remain *in situ*.

I cannot help feeling it should be given decent burial, like a body, for it makes a macabre sight; but at least it will act as a warning to all who pass that way, and I for one know that every time I see it I shall resolve to drive more slowly.

❧

When gamekeepers gather

Listen to – or, as he would say, hark at – this fat gamekeeper with a Berkshire accent complaining to a colleague in the beer tent about the difficulties he had getting his young pheasants back into their pen:

'All went in bar one fucker. You think that little sod'd go through the fuckin' 'ole? Would 'ee buggery! *Nine times* I drives 'im along the wire, and nine times 'ee fuckin' well goes past. In the end I fuckin' left him, didn't I?'

A German friend who had come with me to the Gamekeepers' Fair at Packington Hall, near Coventry, was amazed. 'Why is he using this word all the time?' he asked. 'It makes him feel better,' I said; but, joking apart, I told my friend that what he could hear was the heart of rural England beating strongly.

That is the great attraction of the annual Gamekeepers' Fair, run by the British Association for Shooting and Conservation. Less posh and pretentious than the Game Fair or any of the national agri-cultural shows, it is altogether closer to the earth. When I asked a BASC official if anti-bloodsports agitators ever caused trouble, he replied simply, 'No. There'd be no point, because everyone who comes here understands how the country works.'

This year the day was miraculously fine, and the right note was struck the moment one arrived by the scent of fresh cowpats rising sharp from the sodden grass of the car park. Had the event taken place in the lifetime of D. H. Lawrence, the novelist would have become seriously over-excited, for it attracts gamekeepers by the thousand. However you imagine Lady Chatterley's lover, you would find him here: there are keepers with red beards, with black beards, clean-shaven. Some are tall and straight, some short and bow-legged; some are in tweed suits or moleskin breeches with leather boots and gaiters; others are in camouflage gear from head to foot. There are also a great many wives and children.

On a stall called Country Bygones seventy-seven-year-old Fred Dytham is presiding over a collection of vintage artefacts, among them dozens of ancient shotgun cartridges and a German sniper's telescopic rifle-sight from the First World War. 'I bet when Jerry got that cross on you, you weren't about for long,' says Fred.

Having started at the age of ten, he worked as a keeper in the Midlands all his life; but now, to his disgust, not one of his seven children, fifteen grandchildren and ten great-grandchildren shows the slightest interest in carrying on the family tradition. As if to counter their inertia, Fred himself went on ferreting until last year, killing up to seventy-five rabbits a day with a friend on reclaimed land near Peterborough.

'In the old days, we always used to gut the rabbits straight away,' he says. 'Not now. You don't have to leg 'em or gut 'em or nothing. In fact, the dealer won't have 'em unless the insides are still in. They go away by the ton and finish up in Germany. Now then – I'll tell you: the insides come back as ... ladies' face powder. Careful when you kiss somebody again!'

What better occasion than this for the British Stickmakers' Guild to hold its national competition? Sticks of all descriptions are ranged down the side of a marquee, ready for assessment. For the most elaborate – a showpiece rather than a practical support – you must expect to pay over £100.

One of the judges is Alan Bateman, a driving instructor from Reading, who took last year's trophy with a ram's horn crook decorated with carvings of a blue tit on one side and a bee on the other. The craze for stick-making came over him slowly, he says, but then suddenly took a dangerous grip. 'It became an obsession, I have to admit. It got hold of me to the degree that nothing else in my life mattered. I only had one ambition – to be the best.'

For five years he worked away like a slave in his garage, twenty or twenty-five hours a week. Then at last he felt ready to enter competitions – and began to win. Now, having carried off the national trophy, he is, as he puts it, 'in a phase of rehabilitation' and returning to normal, but still in love with sticks of all descriptions. Ask him about the rival merits of hazel, ash, holly and blackthorn, and his eyes light up.

So do those of Ivan Hancock when you question him about his Purdey among air-rifles, the Venom Mach 1, which is hand-built to order, as supersonic as its name suggests, and makes a vicious crack. When he set up Venom Arms with his partner Dave Pope six years ago, Mr Hancock's aim was to give air-gunners 'weapons they could be proud of'. He began to rebuild production guns to higher specifications and, in so doing, set off a whole new industry. The result is that today's air-weapons bear little resemblance in power or physique to the £25 pop-guns with which most boys were palmed off a generation ago.

The Mach 1 was designed afresh from scratch and, in the words of its creator, its performance is 'far in excess of anything else available'. So is its price – £875 basic, about £1,200 with a good telescopic sight.

And what will a proud owner shoot with this formidable weapon? Perhaps rabbits, squirrels and other vermin, but more likely targets. Here, at one edge of the showground, a whole line of competitors is pinging and zipping away at tin outlines of squirrels, crows and so on, planted in the grass or fastened to the trunks of ancient oaks. Grown men crouch in the mud to aim, oblivious of their surroundings.

From other quarters comes a continual rattle of heavier firing at clay pigeons – the whoosh of black-powder muzzle-loaders and the crackle of modern shotguns. Above the musketry rises the odd yap of a gun-dog on trial and the frantic whistling of its owner.

Suddenly I see a chance of summing up the whole thing for my German friend. 'You know that song,' I say. '"Mad dogs and Englishmen go out in the midday ..."' But just as I am about to utter the fatal word, a clap of thunder bursts above us and down comes the rain.

In the churchyard

The rude forefathers of our hamlet sleep beneath about sixty tomb-stones, many of them tottering with age, and because the churchyard lies on a steep slope, the cutting of the grass between the graves is no straightforward task. Sharing it with a retired farmer, I am frequently embarrassed to find that he has exceeded his norm and done part of my patch before I get there.

Yet it is not this mild dereliction of duty that worries me. What exercises me more is the thought that maybe it is somehow sacrilegious to cut the grass with modern machinery: can it be right to go roaring and whizzing among the graves with hover-mowers and – indispensable adjuncts for all edges – strimmers?

Would *I*, if I were in one of the graves, mind occasional thunderings overhead? I do not think so; it would be more important to know that all was ship-shape above. So I wield the strimmer without too many guilty feelings – even though, at one particular spot, I often get an odd feeling that someone is standing behind me. No doubt it is something to do with the arrangement of the gravestones and the angle at which the sun strikes, for when I turn round, the sensation vanishes, and there is nobody in sight.

Fatal liking for yew

One of the most bizarre recent news items concerned a man who had committed suicide by stuffing himself with yew leaves. His poor wife found him lying in a bath, already dead, but surrounded by pounds more of the greenery that had killed him.

Since the victim was a plant toxicologist, he obviously knew that yew is deadly poisonous; yet it is a curious fact that many animals browse on it without any wish to do themselves in. Although a small amount does them no harm, big doses are fatal.

In deer parks which contain yew trees continuous nibbling usually keeps the foliage at such a height that the deer can only just reach it, and so do not get very much. Trouble sets in either when a large branch is brought down or when a heavy snow-fall lifts the animals to new heights.

A park-keeper once told me that he had found five fallow does dead under a single tree, killed in the night after a sudden orgy made possible by the collapse of a big bough.

On another occasion a gardener, thinking to do the deer in the next-door park a favour, threw the clippings from his yew hedge over the wall – and in the morning seven of the herd's best bucks were stretched out in a line. Sheep are liable to suffer the same fate and even pheasants are for some reason attracted by the little, shiny, pointed leaves.

I am not sure what connection, if any, this has with the free-standing privy at the end of our garden. But ours, like many of the old outdoor lavatories in this part of the world, has an ancient yew tree growing hard by it, and it seems natural to suppose that one was thought to have a beneficial effect upon the other – though in which direction, I cannot find anyone to say.

Who dyes wins

From two miles out the 'Combat Zone' signs guide one in to South Farm at Water Eaton, near Swindon, and there the staff are waiting: four young men and two young women all in identical gear – grey-green, army-type trousers, dark-green sweatshirts emblazoned on the front with the yellow motif 'Combat Zone' and on the back with 'Who dyes wins'.

Like its rival version Skirmish, Combat Zone derives from the American 'Survival' game and the Canadian 'Great Adventure' game. From its first base near Taunton it has now spread to six sites in the south of England and, although its promoters are at pains to point out that it is *not* a war game, it certainly has strong military overtones.

Today's host, Nick Laing, was once a captain in the Scots Guards and now, as a farmer ordered by the Government to cut down food production, he is trying an alternative method of earning income from part of his land. Nature has endowed him with the first essential – a big, thick wood – but already he and his partner have invested £20,000 to get the venture going.

As the players arrive, each is issued with an air-pistol modified to fire gelatine-skinned pellets full of dye, twenty rounds of ammunition, a cartridge belt, a grey overall (in fact an ex-German army tank suit with red, yellow and black flashes still on the upper arms) and a pair of clear protective goggles. There are fifteen men and four women, all in their twenties or early thirties, and all but one from the same computer firm. Each has paid £20, plus VAT, for the day.

Down at the advanced base, outside the wood, tea and coffee are available in an ex-army marquee. In front of it planks ranged on straw bales serve as seats for the main briefing. Already the players have been split into two teams, red and green, distinguished by armbands and, as they wait, high-speed banter, giggling and the occasional discharge of a weapon betray the fact that nerves are on edge. 'Get Jeremy!' someone keeps shouting. 'It doesn't matter what happens, as long as we get Jeremy.'

'The aim of the game is very simple,' Laing tells them. 'Each team has a base, marked by fluorescent tape tied round a group of trees. All you have to do is reach the enemy camp, capture their flag and bring it back to yours. Anyone who gets shot is out of action for the rest of that game and must withdraw into one of the dead-zones...

'Your weapon is a straightforward air-pistol, and it's as dangerous as any air-pistol. Its effective range is about thirty yards. It does *not* work,' he points at one of the girls, 'if you stuff the barrel full of mud. Do *not* deliberately fire at someone's face. Being hit in the face hurts. Aim at the body.

'No climbing of trees, no cutting down of trees. The cover in there's really thick, so it's going to be jungle warfare rather than open warfare ... Enjoy yourselves!'

As we move into the wood, one of the marshals remarks that for the first hour or so both teams will probably blunder about, but that after that they will start working out proper tactics. The unique feature of Combat Zone is its single-shot weapon: whereas other games use pump-guns that can maintain a fusillade, here you need at least five seconds to reload between shots and during that time you are extremely vulnerable. Hence the need to work in pairs, one combatant covering another, and to operate as a team.

Having arrived as an observer, I suddenly find myself co-opted into Red Team, who are a man short. Moments later I am in the jungle with them, armed and visored. The only member of our team who has played before is Jeremy.

'The name of this game's fast loading,' he tells us. 'You've got to load on the run. And when we get there, it's no good hanging about. Fire at them and make them shoot, and then they'll panic like hell.'

A countdown comes through on the radio. A horn blows. Away we go, creeping through head-high nettles, with two defenders left to guard the base. Soon we start to catch glimpses of other grey figures, crouching or slinking among the ash trees. Shots sputter from the undergrowth. People begin to run.

If you want to be disparaging, you can dismiss the whole thing as a form of hide-and-seek for grown-up children. But there is no doubt that it is damned good fun. Primaeval instincts of hunting, hiding, escape and evasion surface in even the most urbanized individuals. Soon men and women alike are plunging through sloughs of liquid black mud and diving into banks of nettles as though they did it every day of their lives. For those who are hit and rendered *hors de combat*, there is some solace in the fact that the dead-zones are equipped with supplies of Mars bars and soft drinks.

The experience of our leader pays off. At lunch the score is 4–1 to us, and everyone is lit up. By the time we gather back at the marquee for a substantial barbecue, office pallor has vanished. Some people are pink in the face, others puce; some have skin as well as clothes stained yellow by the vegetable dye that marks a hit. All are eagerly discussing how best to do down the opposition. In the afternoon the exchanges continue until everyone is exhausted.

Small wonder that several large firms – among them Allied Dunbar, Rothmans and Trustee Savings Bank – have already taken whole days, sending up to fifty young executives to one or other of the Combat Zone sites at the company's expense (the higher the number, the better the battle). So far the aim has been mainly recreational – to give the people concerned an amusing and different day out. But it is clear that the game would make an admirable extension of the extra-mural exercises already used by many companies to evaluate their personnel. A day of combat brings out leadership qualities in striking fashion and welds individuals into a team as few other activities can.

Meanwhile, Nick Laing's immediate ambition is to run his first night game during the full moon in August. So strongly does the idea appeal that 100 people have already applied to participate. How many of them, I wonder, realize that their host's aim – after giving them a slap-up spit-roast supper in the open – will be 'to keep them running for the rest of the night'?

Grey ghost in the valley

Imagine a wooded valley, narrow and deep, cut off from the outside world, with no public right of access. Imagine a chain of five lakes, hemmed in by trees and now much overgrown. And then, at the head of the water, where the valley opens out a little into unkempt pasture land, imagine the grey ghost of a Victorian house hunched against the hillside, with steeply pointed Gothic gables and stone gargoyles in the shape of mythical beasts sprouting horizontally and open-mouthed from the walls above the first-floor windows.

This is Woodchester Park, near Stroud, surely one of the strangest houses in the country, unique in the fact that it was never finished and has never been inhabited by humans. It was begun in about 1854, but towards the end of the 1860s, after fourteen years of leisurely work, it was abandoned by its builders, who departed so precipitately that they left behind their interior scaffolding, ladders and masons' models.

The house was commissioned by William Leigh, the son of a Liverpool merchant, who hired a young local architect called Benjamin Bucknall to design him a country mansion. Bucknall's aim was to build as much as possible in limestone, with the result that the house is not only walled and roofed with stone, but has stone staircases, stone gutters and downpipes, and even a vast stone bath carved from a single block.

With true Victorian extravagance, the house was laid out round a central courtyard, with the kitchen some forty yards from the dining-room. Because Leigh was a man of powerful religious convictions, the building included a chapel thirty feet long with a finely vaulted stone ceiling and splendidly ornate trellised windows.

Although some of the servants' quarters at the back were completed, none of the main apartments except the drawing-room on the ground floor was anywhere near finished, and much of the house has remained to this day a cavernous void three storeys high.

The main beneficiaries have been bats, of which four species have established themselves throughout the structure. (The rarest, the Greater Horseshoe bats, are endangered and therefore of special scientific interest.) Shifting their quarters from roof to cellar and back according to the temperature, and giving their young flying tuition in the corridors, they make free with the generous accommodation and thrive there because the rough meadows opposite, having never

105

been treated with chemicals, harbour a wealth of insects, particularly moths. The bats have been intensively studied over the past thirty years; the adults are all ringed, and one veteran female established an unofficial record by being caught eighty-four times before her death in 1985.

So massive and meticulous was Bucknall's construction that for a century his great pile remained more or less untouched by the weather, and at one stage the domestic quarters were used as class-rooms by a field-study group. At various times it was suggested that the house might become a prison or a lunatic asylum.

In the past twenty years, however, rain has penetrated the roof and vandals have repeatedly broken through the defences erected to block doors and windows. The result is that the building has deteriorated to the point at which it is threatening to collapse in three different places. The chapel is in a particularly dangerous state.

Last year the Victorian Society, which has a keen interest in the house, issued an urgent plea for its preservation, but by then, after many changes of ownership, it was in the hands of an offshore company and there seemed little chance of its being saved. Yet in March this year it was bought – in desperation – by the Stroud District Council, who paid £20,000 for the house and twenty-three acres surrounding it.

All credit to the council for taking on so hungry a white elephant. But what were they to do with it? The easiest alternative – to let it fall down – would clearly have been a form of vandalism far greater than any yet perpetrated. The next best would be to carry out essential repairs, for a further £20,000 – and tenders for these have gone out. But the greatest challenge was to find a long-term use for the place.

To complete the building, tidy up the rotting stonework and put the whole place in livable order would be prodigiously expensive: although no complete survey has been made, it is thought that the price of full restoration would be at least £2 million. But the cost is obviously no deterrent to some people, for of the various offers which the Stroud Council has solicited over the past three months, one was to refurbish the house as a private dwelling and another to turn it into a hotel.

Total restoration, however, is not the aim, for scientific bodies – among them the Nature Conservancy Council – are anxious that the bats should not be evicted, and the Victorian Society is equally keen that the front of the house should remain a shell, with its unique display of Victorian architectural methods and magnificent stone-work visible to posterity. The council, for its part, would like to arrange limited public access.

Some form of partial occupation seems to be the answer, and the Council now thinks it may have found a buyer prepared to cohabit with bats and empty space: a recent meeting of the main planning committee instructed officers to develop one of the schemes proposed. Meanwhile, essential repairs will go ahead anyway, for unless something is done before the winter, one spell of hard frost could bring the chapel roof down.

Whoever he or she may be, the intending purchaser must be a bold spirit. I myself would not live at Woodchester if you paid me for, although its setting is wonderful, the house itself strikes me as full of menace. With its gaunt, unglazed windows, its bare skeleton of stone and above all its gaping gargoyles, the building looks as though it is growling resentment against the humans who have never given it the care that was its due, and I fear that it may make anyone who does now live in it pay the price.

Underground gunnery

It was some time since I had last shot a mole, but earlier this week, in desperation, I was once again driven to the expedient of subterranean gunnery – an art which I first saw practised many years ago by an old woman who stumped about her garden in stout leather boots with a 12-bore in one hand and a pipe in the other.

My victim had a good run. As long as he conducted operations out in the field, I left him alone. It was when he invaded the orchard and garden that relations between us became strained; I could just about stand a few heaps of earth in the rough grass beneath the apple trees, but once he began to undermine the sward below the washing-line and advance under the lawn itself, it became too much.

When I solicited ideas for counter-measures, easily the most futile recommendation came from a neighbour who said that the vibration of horses' hooves would make him decamp, and that I should therefore lead horses about on top of him. Since by now he was well into the lawn, this course did not recommend itself, and in any case he had already made hay (metaphorically speaking) in the field which the horses were grazing.

Strychnine would have done for him, no doubt, but I did not have any by me and do not like the idea of putting poison into the ground. I tried a trap, of course; but, whether by luck or cunning, he never even sprang it. I also tried various locally recommended remedies such as creosote, mothballs and chopped onions poured into his tunnels, none of which made the slightest difference.

Then one evening, as I glanced out of the kitchen window, I saw the ultimate insult – a brand new molehill which had erupted out of a patch of grass mown only that morning. Yet even as I looked at it, outrage turned to hope, for I suddenly saw the earth heave. In a flash I had collected a spade and a shotgun, and taken off my shoes (for moles, being sensitive to vibration, lie doggo if they detect an alien approach). Creeping up the lawn barefoot, I waited to make sure that he was still at work and then, the instant I saw the earth move again, gave him the right-hand barrel from a distance of about three inches, straight down.

The effect was spectacular: the entire heap collapsed into the ground, leaving a small depression. Sometimes a mole thus engaged is momentarily stunned by a near-miss and makes off unless dug out at once, but this time a quick jab with the spade revealed that my tormentor had died instantaneously.

Sorry as I was to have done him in, I felt glad that he had known nothing about it, rather than struggle in a trap or endure agonies of poisoning. If anyone should seek to ridicule the idea of opening up on so small a creature with a 12-bore, I should defend it by saying that it is the most humane method available.

'Take your trousers right off'

'Primarily, the accident areas are from the waist down,' said Bill Jackson, managing director of Hyett Adams, the firm which sells (among other things) chain-saws and garden machinery. 'But the material in this protective suit I'm wearing will certainly reduce the severity of injuries.'

With these cheerful remarks he started a saw, gunned it to full speed and brought the blade down on a spare length of the blue material used in his trousers. Since the demonstration took place in a hotel conference room, the noise was impressive. So was the performance of the cloth, whose long fibres tore out, as they are designed to, and instantly choked the saw to a halt by wrapping themselves round the sprocket that drives the chain.

It was a good gimmick for the launch of new saws and strimmers; but after that opening I spent most of Mr Jackson's talk reflecting on the occasion when, *not* wearing safety trousers as I should have been, I applied a chain-saw lightly to the inside of my knee. The wound, though not incapacitating, obviously needed stitches, so I bound it up and went in search of help.

The nearest telephone was in a pub on the main road; but, this being New Year's Day and the time 2.15, the inmates were not concentrating all that well. When I asked if anyone knew where a doctor would be on duty, they roared with laughter – and I decided that no purpose would be served if I tried to sober them up by showing them that blood was trickling down my right leg into my boot.

In due course I found my way to a country hospital. There the lady doctor on duty greeted me with the irresistible instruction: 'Take your trousers *right off*,' and, as she sewed me up, kept remarking on the fact that my skin was like elephant hide. Thus insult added extra smart to my injury and the memory has not faded. Tempted as I was by the shiny new saws on display last Tuesday, I think I may buy a suit of nylon armour first.

Irish pudding goes off

A quick trip across the water convinced me that the spirit of the Irish RM is alive and well in Co. Tipperary, and that Somerville and Ross would have pounced on a story I heard there.

The wife of a master of foxhounds suddenly decided to throw a grand supper-party, at which the *pièce de résistance* would be a steak and kidney pudding. She therefore went out and bought several pounds of meat, diced it up and put it in a bucket in the larder. Then, however, she lost interest and went off to Dublin for a few days. Returning, she once again addressed herself to the pudding – but by then her ingredients had undergone a sea-change. Mould was growing on the meat and the whole larder smelt dreadful.

Her grown-up stepson besought her to throw the stuff away. 'God, you'll kill us all,' he told her.

'Never,' she said. 'I've made more steak and kidney puddings than you've had hot dinners. It'll be the finest. Away with you.'

Further argument clearly being futile, the young man seized the bucket and dumped its contents down the lavatory next to the kitchen. Inevitably the great lump of steak and kidney blocked the system so solidly that no amount of flushing could shift it.

Now what to do? As the combatants steadied their nerves with a jar or two, it occurred to them that meat will burn. Petrol, then: burn out the blockage. So – a shot of two-star, and *woof*, the curtains were instantly on fire. Only with difficulty did they prevent the blaze spreading to the kitchen.

Another jar or two, and another idea: enlist the help of the hunt terriers, which are small and agile and trained to go down holes. Being permanently half-starved, they would surely eat their way through the obstruction in a trice.

The first dog was tried and performed nobly: having eaten his fill, he came up belching. But with the second, which was smaller and even hungrier – disaster. He went down, but never came up.

'And didn't the poor little devil have to go round the bend!' came the indignant punchline. 'And sure, that was the finish of him.'

At least, they thought it was, for although there was a theoretical possibility that the terrier might have emerged from the far end of the sewer into the bog, the wretched creature was never seen again.

Blackbirds plastered

'Positively no children in the raspberry canes', says the notice at the gate; but even if the owners of the fruit farm can deny access to under-age humans, they cannot keep out the blackbirds, which by now, as the season comes to an end, are more or less grounded by their own excessive consumption.

Although I suppose they must hoist themselves a few feet from the ground to roost – for otherwise the village cats would get them – I really think that during the day they cannot fly at all (and who could, after taking on board the equivalent of several hundred shots

of Framboise?). Instead, they hop silently along the ground from row to row, looking up at the human pickers with a kind of benign stupefaction that puts me in mind of Chas, our local brewer, after a night on his Old Spot ale.

I myself never feel so relaxed in a pick-your-own establishment: the atmosphere is too competitive and I am kept on edge by the nagging fear that other people may be finding better patches than I am – even though experience repeatedly confirms that it is pointless to worry. Because everyone is of a slightly different size and shape, and inclined at a slightly different angle to the universe, no two people have the same view of a line of raspberry canes. The result is that when one picker has worked a row, another can follow along and do just as well.

Among new arrivals the tension is generally too great for conversation, but as baskets start to fill and it becomes apparent that there is plenty of fruit for everybody, a relaxed mateyness spreads through the company. Some people chat directly to strangers. Others, fancying that they are out of earshot, mutter and exclaim to themselves. Others again let out an intermittent barrage of comments that may or may not be designed to provoke answers.

One day this week, as I picked in T-shirt and jeans, I became aware of an improbable-looking competitor in the next-door line: thin, seventyish, ramrod straight, sweltering in a loud tweed suit and cap – a retired army officer, if ever I saw one. Sure enough, his voice was as military as his manner. After a few clearing shots of 'Perfectly ridiculous!' he said gruffly, 'Trouble is, with the damn great freezers one has nowadays, you never see these things again once they've gone in. Don't know what my wife does with them.'

Not feeling confident of producing a sensible riposte, I sidled on up my row. Then a minute or two later I saw the maroon grid-lines of his suit looming through the foliage straight opposite.

'Do better at this job if you had four pairs of hands,' he muttered.

'And four pairs of eyes,' I answered.

'Ha!'

And so a sporadic conversation began, none of it initiated by me.

'They ought to give you some sort of thing you could hang round your neck to put 'em in. Damn sight easier.'

'Absolutely.'

'Looks as though a herd of buffalo's been through here . . .'

'I know.'

'Get out, you brute [to a blackbird]... Place is alive with 'em, cheeky beggars.'

'I think they're all plastered.'

'Who are?'

'The birds.'

This observation seemed to unsettle him. At any rate, he fell silent. But a few minutes later I heard, 'Twelve o'clock. Time for a glass of sherry. Clean your palate with a few of these, nice and sharp, and the sherry goes down a treat. Just the job.'

With that he stumped off. I was sorry to see him go, but when I looked down at my basket, I found it was almost full. Hastened by our staccato and unpredictable exchanges, time (unlike the blackbirds) had flown.

Lament for a lost world

Driving up the lovely strath of Kildonan, in Sutherland, I got a strange and unpleasant shock. For some miles I had been thinking fondly of a substantial Victorian shooting lodge called Suisgill, over-looking the Helmsdale river, which I had often visited in times gone by as a guest of the owner, Lady Paynter.

By the time I knew her, she was of substantial age and dimensions: I see her especially steaming up the mountain on a stout Garron pony, looking like a Highland Boadicea in her rig of deer-stalker hat and voluminous grey tweed cape. But she was a marvellously gen-erous hostess, inviting a succession of young men to shoot her grouse and stags or catch her salmon, and not the least of her achievements was to have created a glorious garden in a landscape which normally supports nothing but rough grass and heather.

Imagine my dismay, therefore, when at last I reached the place, only to find the house clean gone, the garden vanished away. Too late I remembered a rumour that the lodge had been burned down by vandals. Now I found not only that the story was true, but that almost every trace of the building had been erased. Only a scar on the hillside marked its site, and another graze the place where I had once seen lupins and roses blazing.

Yet the disappointment brought back vivid memories of Lady Paynter herself, and in particular of her celebrated apricot poodle, Waffle. The great accomplishment of this creature – in his owner's eyes – was that he had learned to retrieve grouse, a skill not normally acquired by members of his breed.

If the truth be told, Waffle did not retrieve very well. When a grouse was shot, he would certainly charge towards the fallen bird, urged on by stentorian contralto hoots of 'Good boy, Waffle! On you go!' But once he had found the quarry, his interest quickly waned and, after giving the bird a good bite or two (which usually disembowelled it there and then), he would come prancing back over the heather without it.

This habit by no means endeared him to Lady Paynter's head keeper, Donald, a splendid professional whose own retrievers were highly trained. Whenever the poodle frisked into action, Donald would utter the most frightful curses, calling for the animal's sudden extermination. 'Shoot the f…r!' he would cry, in extremities of vexation and then, as yet another grouse was rendered unfit for the table, he would give a terrible groan of, 'Oh, buggering hell!'

In fact there was no physical action that could be taken, for in the Paynter establishment Waffle was top dog, and Donald knew it better than anyone – as a single immortal utterance confirmed.

One day we were out after grouse and it had been arranged that at lunchtime Lady Paynter would ride up to join us, bringing our picnic in the panniers of her horse. At about ten to one, as we came down over a wide sweep of heather towards the path on which she would appear, I found myself next to Donald in the line and asked him if it was still safe to shoot in front.

'Carry on,' he said. 'You're quite all right. I don't mind if you shoot her ladyship, *but for Christ's sake don't shoot Waffle.*'

Barrage in the suburbs

My instructor is Roland Wild, an ex-farmer from St Albans, solid and genial, endowed with the priceless gift of being able to praise or blame without seeming unctuous or carping and of always being able to put a customer at ease, no matter how great fool he may be making of himself.

'You were eighteen inches below that bird,' he says as yet another clay target wings on its way untouched. 'You brought the gun very high on the cheek. Not quite enough front hand. Try another.'

We are on the driven grouse stand at the Holland & Holland shooting school near Northwood, on the western fringes of London. Thirty yards out in front and slightly above us, our trapper Paul (who sports one gold ear-stud) is working three traps concealed behind a hedge, so that as he ranges up and down unseen the clays come whizzing in pairs from a variety of angles.

Had I been a beginner, I would first have had a twenty-minute talk on safety and then fired a couple of shots at a mark on a steel plate to make sure that I had the gun lined up correctly; but since I am fairly experienced, we have come straight to the driven grouse, which are upon us in a flash.

'This is *not* a place to start a novice,' says Roland cheerfully as he blows the whistle for Paul to let fly. Only a faint thud betrays the fact that the trap has sprung, and suddenly another pair of clays is skimming at us. Gradually I get the hang of letting instinct take control – for there is no time to think or plan. After thirty rounds rapid, the barrels are too hot to touch except through the leather hand-guard.

We move to one of the high towers, where Paul climbs 115 feet to an armoured crow's nest in an oak tree. Launched at that height, the targets look like dots in the sky. 'What do I do here?' I ask – and the answer is, 'Hope!'

The shooting grounds are an extraordinary enclave – a forty-acre oasis of fields and tall hedges bang (as you might say) in the middle of the packed suburbia of Ruislip and Northwood. The facilities include a 100-yard range on which one can fire the big-game rifles for which the firm is famous.

The texture of the soil must by now be very odd, for at this, the height of the season, it is repeatedly top-dressed with lead pellets at the rate of some 1,500 lbs a week. Empty cartridge cases are raked up and burned, and groups of boy scouts come in once a month to carry off all the unbroken clays they can find, but the fields are carpeted with the remains of shattered targets, which gradually work down into the grass. Occasionally the firm sends off samples of soil for analysis, but the only treatment needed, apparently, is a dressing of crushed limestone.

In spite of the continuous gunfire, the place is teeming with wildlife. Because the grass is never sprayed, it harbours a wealth of insects and these in turn attract birds, which regard the ceaseless volleys as no more than soothing background noise. Woodpeckers, tree-creepers, nuthatches, whitethroats, warblers, owls, kestrels and sparrowhawks carry on as though in the depths of the country – and things become even more realistic when the occasional gunner, carried away by his own prowess at the clays, downs a live pigeon that has recklessly ventured into the school's air space.

Whether or not one is about to go game-shooting, a lesson is highly entertaining – and so, you might think, it had better be, for by the time you have paid for an hour's instruction, cartridges and clay targets, it costs literally a guinea a minute. Many people come without any ulterior motive, merely to enjoy themselves, and some – women as well as men – become so addicted that they buy season tickets.

One of the fascinations of taking a lesson is that an intimate connection is quickly established between teacher and pupil. The instructor, standing right behind you, can see the shot as it flies through the air and is so immediately involved that he seems able to divine your every thought.

'I get such a close rapport with some people that the shot they are firing becomes *my* shot,' says Ken Davies, the red-haired, red-bearded chief instructor who has been with Hollands for twenty-one years. 'You wouldn't believe how often I get accused of mind-reading.'

Being probably the most experienced coach in the world, Mr Davies is in keen demand. He goes on coaching trips to America twice a year and during the winter (if you book early enough) you can hire him to come and steady your nerves in the shooting field itself for the modest fee of £350 a day.

At the school the trend is now strongly towards corporate shoots, in which a firm takes over the whole place for a morning or afternoon. Whereas (in Mr Davies's estimation) a company outing to Wimbledon or the races is essentially passive entertainment, this is very much action for everyone, in which 'people who've never even seen a shotgun jump in and have a go'. After a gentle introduction, even beginners become mustard-keen, especially in the grand blast-off at the end – a flush of 100 targets pouring over in only a couple of minutes.

Some of them, however, need firm handling. During one corporate day a man who had not shot much before kept ignoring safety advice and persistently let his loaded gun point down towards his feet. In the end Mr Davies suddenly fired both barrels into the ground just in front of him, blowing two large holes in the turf.

'Heavens!' I said. 'Did that improve things?'

'Oh, yes,' said the chief instructor. 'It made him concentrate.'

Rifle fire at midnight

The dinner-party ended as all country dinner-parties should – in a flurry of disorganization and excitement.

Our hosts had recently bought the central portion of a substantial house, and during the evening they explained that relations were not altogether easy with their neighbours, X and Y, who owned either end of the building. It was not that these two had any particular disagreement with the newcomers: rather, they had for some time been feuding with each other.

One of X's standard ploys, when wanting to assert himself, was to turn off the water (over which, unfortunately, he had control), and sure enough he did this in the course of dinner. But our hostess received the news that the taps had run dry with equanimity, for it had often happened before and she had laid in reserve supplies.

It was not until the meal had ended and the party was about to break up that events took a lively turn. Then at midnight rifle shots began to go off outside the house. Our host went out to investigate. Conversation had been flowing, but now – punctuated by the occasional further report – it became a little strained.

We hung on for a while, but by about 12.30 we felt we must go. When our hostess opened the front door to show us out, there, capering crazily in the rain, was a bizarre threesome. The principal figure was Y, clad in a camouflage smock, manifestly plastered, grappling with a woman and still clutching in one hand the .22 with which he had been loosing off at X's upper windows. Grappling with both man and woman, and trying to manoeuvre them into the kitchen, where he felt they would be less of a menace, was our host.

'Got to get some black coffee down him,' we heard him mutter. Understandably, our protestations of gratitude seemed to lack conviction. I felt I should offer to help, but then thought, no – this is a private affair and none of my business. So we drove away into the rain, with the trio of combatants moving jerkily in an erratic, crabwise shuffle towards the lighted doorway.

Less than a quarter of a mile from the house we came on two police cars parked beside the road. Hell, I thought, this is finally it. But no – they paid no attention and I suddenly realized that they were poised to move in on the midnight gunman.

A check-up next day revealed that they had arrived within minutes of our departure and taken Y into custody. Next day, in his absence, his girlfriend rushed in to our friends to say that the house was on fire – as indeed it was. A mysterious blaze had broken out at the point where the electric supply enters the building.

Now, with Y banned from the premises by court order until his case comes up, things have settled down a bit, but I cannot help feeling glad that I do not live sandwiched between two such volatile and fractious neighbours.

Main course in flames

The incident brought back another evening made memorable by an unscheduled interruption. We had gone to dine in a neighbouring farmhouse. During the first course our hostess glanced to her left through the open doorway, gave an explosive shriek and dashed out into the kitchen.

'Typical Frenchwoman,' I said to myself. 'Over-reacting as usual,' But when I got up and had a look, all I could see was dense black smoke and through it, dimly visible, flames leaping.

We sprang into action. The husband, realizing that what had caught fire was a pan of oil left on the stove to heat for the main course of *fondue*, and that the flames were about to engulf an electric power-point above the stove, sensibly pulled the main switches and plunged the whole house into darkness.

By throwing damp blankets over the blaze, we put it out – but not before our clothes, hair and faces had been smothered with greasy black smuts. Although not much damage had been done, the worst insult came when the power was switched on again. Light revealed that the stairs and landing, which before the conflagration had looked immaculately white, now resembled some rarely used hideaway of Count Dracula, being festooned by immense black cobwebs, every filament of which was picked out with soot.

We ate some cheese and tried in vain to convince our hostess that the evening had been rendered unforgettable – as indeed it had. She, poor soul, was hysterical at the ruination of her plans; but I have always thought that it was not the absence of any main course which upset her, so much as the emergence of those nightmare cobwebs and the revelation that her housework was not all that it might have been.

Cross-country cattle

By this stage of the summer a combination of heat and damp has brought forth a plague of flies in woods and fields, particularly along hedgerows frequented by cattle, and no doubt it is the goading of these insects that has provoked a series of escapes.

First a bunch of steers broke out of their field, charged through the wood and picked up a dairy herd as they trotted along a lane. Soon the whole lot arrived in high spirits on the village green, where they caused no small amount of damage to gardens. By the time the invaders had been repelled, their owners were not popular.

Two evenings later, at about 7.30, I happened to glance out of the kitchen window and saw two hefty bullocks saunter past, pausing only to munch the hollyhocks that grow inside our wall. By means of a rapid deployment we managed to trap them in a neighbour's farmyard, but they were clearly the scouts of some bigger party, and a few telephone calls established that nine more were at large elsewhere.

Back-tracking along the spoor, I came on the signs of a merry charge: deep, splayed footmarks showed that the main bunch had gone through the wood at a gallop, and dusk was falling before we caught up with them. By then they had pushed their way into another farmer's field and joined forces with some thirty others. With the light failing, it was impossible to weed out the runaways from the rest, so we had to leave them till morning.

Both these manoeuvres were tiresome and time-consuming, yet neither was anything like as ridiculous as a sequence of events in which my sister recently found herself caught up. The culprit in this case was a single steer which had already proclaimed its escapist tendencies by breaking out of its own field and travelling three miles across country; but, since it then settled down among some cattle belonging to my sister, she and its owner, Reg, decided to leave it for the duration.

Trouble set in when he arrived, several months later, to take it home. The animal recognized him at once and by no means fancied what it saw. Having taken one look, it lit off at a gait that can only be described as derisive: head up, tail up, back legs flicking out rigidly in a springing trot.

For the next four hours it was pursued across country by a pack of humans, often five strong. Whenever it came to a barbed-wire fence, it did not look for a gap, as saner cows do, but burst straight through. Cottage gardens offered no greater obstacle: it ploughed through them too, with the proprietors gaping open-mouthed.

Its one potentially serious mistake was to enter a double garage, of which it carried out a brief inspection. At that very moment a woman drove up in a car containing two Dalmatians; but even though the pursuers – who by then were very close – roared at her to slam the garage doors, her reactions were far too slow and in a flash the steer was away again.

At one stage it seemed to tire and lay down for a rest among other cattle. Reg – by then in extremities of exasperation – took a rush and a dive at it, but in the mêlée found that he had dropped with a stranglehold on the wrong animal. Off again, the animal was finally brought to bay in a farmyard hastily barricaded with large pieces of machinery. Cornered at last, it began to charge everybody in sight, until Reg gave it one over the head with a length of cast iron pipe. The blow stunned it sufficiently for five humans, cursing prodigiously, to grapple with it, get a halter round its neck and bundle it into a truck.

The strangest features of the whole performance were, first, that nobody lodged a complaint (even though several gardens had been trampled), and second, that after forcing passage through more than thirty barbed-wire fences, the animal had not a scratch on it. It seemed to have been armoured by its own infuriation, one onlooker describing it as literally rigid with rage.

Later, when Reg took it to market, he did not mention its amazing cross-country performance – but he did take the precaution of driving right into one of the pens before opening the tailboard of his lorry.

Le ménace actuel

After flies and escaping cattle, the worst curse of our summer is the trickle of visitors who fail to comprehend that narrow country lanes call for a special kind of driving. It does not seem to strike them that if the road is seven feet wide, with head-high banks on either hand, there is absolutely no room for manoeuvre. Nor can they understand – until they have been steadied by a head-on crash – that no vehicle descending a one-in-four gradient at speed can stop in its own length, especially in the rain.

For the past few days *le ménace actuel*, as they themselves would call it, has been a French family whose *père* drove up and down at forty miles per hour with one hand on the horn. I daresay he was not very pleased one morning to find in his car an anonymous note saying that, if he continued thus, he would kill someone, preferably himself; and now I expect he has gone home bursting with the news that this part of England is inhabited by rebarbative lunatics. If he has, I do not mind, for with any luck he feels so chagrined that he will not come again.

The beasts of Exmoor

To Exmoor, to fancy the Beast – or rather the Beasts, for it is now clear that the moor itself and the rolling farmland on its southern and south-western fringes are tenanted not by one large, catlike animal, but by several. So many people have seen big predators that, even though much about them remains mysterious, it is no longer possible to doubt their existence.

The trail leads a visitor straight to eye-witnesses. Listen to Paget King-Fretts, a retired farmer with a lifetime's experience of animals (including leopards in India during the war) whose cottage is tucked away in a valley east of South Molton. One evening in September 1983 he went out at six o'clock to close the gate that leads from his garden into the wood behind.

'There, about forty paces off on the mown grass ride, sat this huge, jet-black cat, facing me. It had a round face and little pointed ears. It was the colour of a Labrador – but you know how a dog's nose and jaw stick forward. This had a round, flat face, and immediately I thought, "God, this is the Beast ..." '

Listen to Mervyn Nicholls, a hard-headed farmer in the same area, whose family has lost several sheep, all killed by having their throats bitten out: 'There's several different animals around, different colours. We know there's a grey-blue, we know there's a black, we know there's one with brown on it. The ones we've seen all have long, flying tails. We've seen them taking fantastic leaps – they could go straight over that hedge there easily.'

Listen to Trevor Beer, a naturalist from Barnstaple, who has written a whole booklet on the phenomenon. In 1984, drawn to investigate a particular wood by the fact that carcases of red deer had been found there, he had just crossed a small stream when he looked up the opposite slope of the valley.

'The head and shoulders of a large jet-black animal appeared out of the bushes only thirty paces off. Its head was broad and sleek with small ears, and its eyes were clear greeny-yellow. As it stared back at me, I noticed its thick neck, powerful forelegs and deep chest. Then, without a sound, it turned and moved swiftly away through the trees.'

Instinctively Mr Beer went after it. By the time he gained the edge of the wood, it was moving off at speed across the field outside, forelegs pushing back between hindlegs, and it disappeared with a flying leap that took it through the top of a high hedge. To Mr Beer, the animal was undoubtedly some form of black panther, about two feet tall at the shoulder and four feet long in the body, and weighing at least 100 lbs.

It is now twenty years since large tracks began to be found, and eight years since regular sightings were first reported. Activity rose to fever pitch early in 1983, when Eric Ley, who farms at Drewstone (also near South Molton), had more than eighty sheep killed in only three months. Such was the slaughter that a detachment of Royal Marines was called in and two-man teams lay out night after night trying to shoot the marauder. They were said to have wounded one animal, which they never accounted for; but, although their efforts took the pressure off Drewstone, sightings have continued intermittently ever since and farmers are still losing sheep every week.

In the early days many people believed that the killers were dogs, but now all the evidence suggests that they are cats. Tracks, hair, gait and habits all seem to be feline. One farmer found wool in the branches of a tree directly above a kill. Another man watched for

ten minutes as a black creature like a panther stalked a sheep, creeping, rising and settling in entirely catlike fashion before making a final spring. A tuft of hair from another kill was definitely identified as that of a lynx. Many people have heard catlike screams at night, often antiphonal, as if one caller is answering another.

Tantalizing questions recur. Do the animals have lairs? If they do, why has none been found? If they are breeding, why has no one seen a cub? Why have no remains been discovered? Why has nobody been able to shoot, catch or photograph a single specimen? How many are there? Above all, how did they come to be on Exmoor?

This last question is perhaps the easiest to answer. If they are panthers, pumas or lynxes (or possibly hybrids), they or their ancestors must have escaped or been released from zoos, circuses or private menageries. Strong rumours circulate that a former butcher in Barnstaple, now in gaol in America, let go two pumas, one brown, one nearly black, when ordered by the police to dispose of them in 1976.

Far from being a joke or gimmick, the Beasts are regarded as a menace. So far they have posed no threat to humans, but they are taking steady toll of sheep and their presence makes it difficult for farmers to let grazing. Nor is it easy to see what can be done about them; so far they have evaded all attempts at shooting, and even if one were killed, it would not end their reign – though of course a body would be of immense zoological interest.

Nobody has studied the phenomenon more closely than Nigel Brierley, a retired biologist living near Bishops Nympton, in the heart of the Beasts' main territory. Working with farmers, vets, police and the local hunts, he has collected evidence for twenty years and now, from close analysis of kills, believes that his own area is frequented by at least five different animals. Further, he believes (from the weight of meat eaten off single kills) that one pair had cubs last summer, but that for some reason they have not produced offspring this year.

His own secret weapon is a large plot of catmint, specially grown for the production of oil, with which he hopes to lure one of the big cats to a point where he can catch or film it. But he emphasizes that the scale of the search is really beyond local means: he needs expensive, sophisticated equipment such as image-intensifiers for night vision, and above all he is anxious that people should take the problem seriously.

Shades of Colonel Hawker

When the men of Longparish, in Hampshire, take the field at Lord's on Monday for the final of the National Village Cricket competition against the Yorkshire team of Treeton, how many of them will be thinking of their illustrious predecessor, Colonel Peter Hawker, who lived from 1786 to 1853? Not many, I wager, for although the Colonel's books are immortal and still in print, he was not a cricketer, but a shooting man, who saw the summer as a tedious period which had somehow to be endured before he could once again open up on the partridges and pheasants which then abounded in the fields around Longparish. To him the finest date in the calendar was 1 September, the start of the partridge season.

He lived in a lovely house (which still stands) overlooking the river Test, some four miles west of Andover, and during the summer months would ease his frustration by killing trout – an activity about which, as about his shooting, he boasted atrociously in his journal. Soldier, farmer, author and inventor, he became such an authority on firearms that he was received by Queen Victoria and Prince Albert, and was also passionately fond of music.

The great feature of Hawker's writing is its vigour. 'On like a mad dog from morning to night with Colonel Shrapnel, my old friend,' reads a typical entry in his diary. Or again, after an outing in France: 'Finished the day with shooting my dog, at the express desire of Mrs Hawker, and to the great satisfaction of all who were with us.'

He reminds me of a pressure-cooker on high heat: blasts of sarcasm and indignation roar out like steam escaping through the safety valve. His temper, already choleric, was sharpened by the wound which he sustained at the battle of Talavera in the Peninsula War, and which troubled him intermittently ever afterwards; and nobody can ever have harboured a more fiercely competitive streak.

Thus he feuded for years with a 'green-livered lawyer' whose only crime was to shoot on a next-door beat, and his account of the poaching raid on Parson Bond's coverts is a classic:

> The scene of confusion was ridiculous beyond anything, and the invasion of an army could scarcely exceed the noise. Not a word could be heard for the cries of 'Mark!', 'Dead!' and 'Well done!' interspersed every moment with *bang bang* and the yelping of barrack curs.... The parson at last mustered his whole establishment to act as patriots against the marauders, footboys running one way, ploughmen mounted on carthorses galloping the other, and everyone from the village that could be mustered was collected to repel the mighty shock....
>
> The parson, having eased himself with a vomit, began to speak more coherently, and addressed himself to those who, being liable to an action of trespass, were obliged to stand on the footpath and take the birds as they came over.

The Colonel records that 1 September 1837 – exactly 150 years ago – was cold and stormy. Nevertheless he bagged twenty-four partridges and two hares without a miss, and 'made seven brilliant double shots. In all my life I never shot better ... in short the performance was perfection.' Next day, out again, he made 'five glorious doublets of the greatest difficulty'.

Modesty was not one of his failings. But if some of the zest and confidence with which Hawker went about killing things can somehow infect the cricketers of Longparish when they go to Lord's, they will make mincemeat of the men from the north. He himself had a house in London, and would certainly have turned out to support the village on their great day. Somehow I have a feeling his spirit will be with them.

Kitchen invaders

The brutes must look through the telephone book and try anyone who lives on a farm. There is no other explanation. They assume – not without reason – that many farmhouses still have primitive kitchens, and simply dial the number.

'This is Alpha Kitchens,' said the girl. 'We happen to be in your area today. Are you thinking of having a new kitchen built?'

What I *should* have said, in a thick local burr, was, 'Am I buggery!' As it was, I hesitated, weakened and agreed to see a Mr Bloggs at 4 pm.

'It'll take him at least two hours to draw up a proper plan,' the girl warned me.

'That's all right. Shall I tell you how to find us?'

'No, no – he's got a map.'

In fact we *had* been thinking about refurbishing the kitchen, but as a dream project rather than as an immediate practical possibility; and so in a way we looked forward to Bloggs's arrival. This took place not at 4 but at 5.35 and, when he at last pulled into the yard, he was muttering darkly abut his lack of directions. Had he come from X, I asked, naming the town in which the girl had said Alpha was operating? Not at all. He was from Y, quite the other direction.

The cover story was blown straight away. By then we were not feeling very receptive, having hung about for ninety minutes. The opening exchanges were thus rather cool. Gradually, however, a sensible plan emerged. Things began to look promising.

The fridge could be fitted into the central work-unit; there would still be space for a dog-bed beside the stove. Even the fact that the stone-flagged floor drops steeply did not throw Mr Bloggs at all: his units, he said, had extending feet, which could easily deal with the fall.

At last, around 8 pm, we reached the question of price. Alpha, our man explained, held costs to rock bottom by not having any showrooms. Hence everything was amazingly cheap. After a few last punches on his calculator he announced that our beautiful new kichen would cost only ... £6,000. Besides, if we put down a deposit of £50 (refundable should we decide not to go ahead), he could guarantee to hold that price for a year.

I paid the £50 as much to get Bloggs on his way as to secure the deal. Next day he telephoned to ask when we proposed to proceed.

I repeated what I had already told him several times – that we could not afford to go ahead in the foreseeable future and would have to wait for an improvement in our finances. Two days later, his manager rang to say that he did not understand the delay. He did a moment later.

But scarcely was he off the line when on came Beta Kitchens, and we began to go through the whole performance again, almost verbatim. This time we decided to endure it for the sake of making a comparison.

Mr Scroggs was older, more amusing, more deft in conversation. The design he produced – though he did not know it – was practically identical with Bloggs's; but *his* price was nearly £9,000, which would be reduced to £6,000 if we went ahead in the next fortnight, because Beta happened to be running a special discount scheme. A cheque for £100 would secure the price indefinitely . . .

Next morning his boss telephoned to ask when we proposed to sign a deal. We told him we could not commit ourselves for the moment. As I put the receiver down, the telephone rang again. 'Gamma Kitchens here,' said a voice. 'We happen to be in your area today . . .'

'*No!*' I said.

'What?' The young man sounded pained as well as startled. 'Let me just tell you that our firm has no showrooms, so that prices are exceptionally low . . .'

'Sorry,' I said, 'no deal.' That was the end of him. But it will not be the end of the nuisance. How do I stop them? Only, I fear, by changing my entry in the telephone book, so that it looks as though I live in a high-rise block of flats rather than on a farm.

Through Indian eyes

The Indian friends whom we had invited to stay kept apologizing. 'We're wasting so much of your time,' they said whenever I took them for a walk or to look at some curiosity nearby. In fact they were doing the very opposite. Not only were they giving us the fun of their company: they were also opening my eyes to my own surroundings in a way that I could scarcely have imagined.

To me, the environment in which Balram and Mira live, on the edge of the jungle near the Nepalese border, is immensely strange and exciting. At night you can hear tigers roaring and with any luck you will see one come to a kill at dusk or dawn. There are bears, leopards, monkeys, porcupines, jackals, several kinds of deer and miraculous numbers of birds. In clear weather the eternal snows of the Himalayas stand out above the forest on the northern skyline.

Compared with this exotic paradise, our own environment seems very tame. Our animals are small, our birds few, our hills almost invisible by Himalayan standards. Yet my friends came into it with cries of pleasure, exclaiming at the texture of land and buildings and vegetation. Being experienced practical naturalists, they could compare every aspect of the country with what they knew at home.

'Show me an oak tree,' said Mira. 'I must get a proper idea of what an oak is like' – and when I found her one, she was delighted by its strength. Wood pigeons – commonplace to me – excited her special admiration because they are so much bigger than Indian doves. To glimpse a jay, and be able to say that she had seen one, quite made her day. A fox, to her, would have been quite as good as a tiger. Balram, meanwhile, brought back a glowing report of how he had come across three grey squirrels gathering hazel nuts in a hedge.

Such enthusiasm was infectious. I started to see everything afresh, and to appreciate how interesting our own small country is. After a couple of days I felt that it was I, and not the Indians, who had been on holiday.

Suicide mission in Wiltshire

One would hardly expect the country town of Bradford-on-Avon, with its mellow stone houses set steeply on the hills, to be the scene of a kamikaze air-strike. Wiltshire, after all, is some way from the Persian Gulf. Nevertheless, an attack that ended in suicide did take place there recently.

Some friends of ours, on a visit to a pet shop, were greatly taken by a pair of gouldians – exotic finches now bred in this country, but originally from the tropical rainforests of Australia, whose colouring is so brilliant and clear cut that it looks as though it had been painted on by a child: red head, black cape, bright lavender bib, yellow belly and black tail. Although the price was appalling – £55 for the pair –

our friends could not bear to see them languishing in a small cage, and bought them.

At home they already had a large aviary full of finches in the garden, but the newcomers, needing a minimum temperature of 60°, were given five-star accommodation in a 6′ by 3′ flight or enclosure in the sun-room on the patio. There they settled in well and all went smoothly until the third day after their arrival.

Then, at teatime, the lady of the house heard a sudden commotion and rushed out to find the gouldians going berserk with fright and a sparrowhawk thrashing its wings against the glass wall of the patio. As she appeared, the raider took off and flew away, but by then both finches were stretched out horizontally in the wood shavings on the floor.

Whether they were instinctively playing possum or grounded by heart-failure, their owner could not tell. The second alternative seemed more likely, for the birds are highly strung, but, when she rang to consult her husband, who was at work, he suggested she leave them alone to see what would happen. Sure enough, after an hour the hen came round, and twenty minutes later her mate also surfaced, none the worse.

Three days later, as the owner sat reading the paper and having a morning coffee, she was startled by the single loud thud of a big bird striking the glass. Again she rushed out. This time the attacker had come in so fast, under the radar (as it were), at low level over the car-port, that the finches had not even seen it and were quite unmoved.

Not so the sparrowhawk, which the woman found lying on the ground, barred breast uppermost, breathing its last. As she picked it up, its eyelids fluttered, and she was startled by the brilliance of its amber eyes, in which life still flickered. Altogether, she was overcome by the beauty of what she called 'this incredible flying machine', which had come to an ignominious end, yet was unmarked by its head-on impact with the glass. Wrapping it in a towel, she put it in a shoe-box and took it to the nearest surgery, but the vet pronounced it dead on arrival.

Where it had come from remains a mystery, for the garden is one of many in the middle of a housing estate and some way from any wood. But clearly the hawk had been fascinated by the garish plumage of the gouldians; and it was the promise of an exceptional, £55 meal which, in spite of the frustration of its first sortie, lured it back three days later to its doom.

Two with one shot

During a week's deer-stalking in the Western Highlands I fired only one shot – but it proved such a prodigious fluke that I feel it should not go unrecorded.

Between torrential showers, which were being blasted in from the west by a gale, we stalked the same stag for nearly two hours. He was feeding along a steep face in the company of a few hinds and kept moving on above us on our left. To stay out of the deer's sight, we had to scramble awkwardly along the edge of a burn, in and out the water.

At last the lie of the hill enabled us to turn left and start climbing towards our quarry. Beneath a single 200-year-old Scots pine – gallant survivor of the Caledonian forest – we left sticks, my telescope and Pansy the Labrador in the charge of a ghillie, and set out on our final approach in a belly crawl through deep heather.

By the time we reached a suitable firing point, at a range of 200 yards, the stag had lain down so that only his antlers were visible. After waiting for another storm to go through, the stalker gave a whistle to put him up. At the sound the beast looked round, stood up, walked a few paces to his left and stopped.

'That'll do,' whispered the stalker. 'Take him there.'

I fired. The stag collapsed instantaneously and rolled a few yards down the steep slope towards us, stone dead. From the way he fell, I knew I had hit him in the neck rather than the heart, where I had been aiming – so here at once was a fluke, a poor shot undeservedly effective.

As we went up, we loosed the dog, who cast about, picked up the scent and eventually sat down on the spot where the stag had been standing.

'She's found the blood where he fell,' the stalker said, and I agreed, although I felt slightly puzzled, as the bitch's normal habit is to sit by the body itself. When we gralloched the stag, Pansy did come down to receive a titbit of liver, but still I sensed that something was odd.

We were fastening ropes on to the stag, about to pull it down to the glen track, when my subconscious doubts rose to the surface and I announced that I was going up to make sure I had not shot another animal too. Only ten yards above us, out of sight in a hollow, I found a hind lying dead. By a million-to-one chance a fragment of the .300

magnum bullet, emerging from the stag's neck, had hit her smack between the eyes.

It was both a disaster (for the hind was out of season) and a miracle. In almost twenty years on the hill the stalker had known nothing like it. If we had realized that the hind was in line, we would have waited until the stag moved clear; but neither of us had had the faintest idea that she was there, and the only consolation was that she, equally, cannot have had the faintest notion that anything was amiss. The one character who came out of the incident with honour was Pansy, but for whom we would have left £60-worth of venison to rot on the hill.

In the wilderness

'There's the pub train away,' said Chris McLeod, our stalker, resignedly as a long, single hoot floated up to us from the glen a thousand feet below. A few moments later we heard the 18.36 from Corrour rattle off southwards towards its next stop seven miles down the line at Rannoch.

The sight of the train, crawling far below us like a caterpillar through the desolate wastes of north-west Inverness-shire, brought home with full force the emptiness of the Highlands. In an age when much of Britain has been overrun by development, deer forests like Corrour are still almost unimaginably remote. Admittedly the cluster of houses at the eastern end of Loch Ossian is connected with the main road by a fifteen-mile gravel track, but the place has no telephone or mains electricity and lies beyond the reach of any television transmitter. The post is brought up five miles from the railway three times a week by the station-master's wife, who hurtles about like some latterday Boadicea on a cross-country tricycle. If the lodge caught fire (as it twice has in the past) help could not arrive in less than two and a half hours.

For Chris and his fellow stalkers, the sole practical means of finding entertainment in the evenings is to board the train for a drink at the Rannoch Hotel. The snag is that the timetable allows them only ninety minutes in the pub on weekdays, and forty on Sundays, before the last train home.

Fortunately the bar windows command a good view of the line, so that in clear weather patrons can see the train labouring up the gradient some way off and have time to drink up before briskly walking the 300 yards or so to the platform. Trouble sets in when the mist comes down: if word suddenly goes up that the train has arrived unseen, a mad dash is needed.

A cynic might say that the stalkers have nothing to worry about: a 300-yard sprint, a ten-minute train ride and a five-mile drive pass quickly enough after a few drams. So they do – at most times of the year. But when winter closes in and the track to the station is blocked, visits to the bar are snuffed out by the snow.

Corrour Halt could hardly be called a jewel among stations. Apart from the signal block, the only building is a single house beside the line, set in a sea of mud paddled flat by geese, who follow their owner indoors and out at will. All around stand wheel-less wrecks of vehicles and heaps of scrap metal.

Nevertheless, the place is not without interest. At 1,350 feet, the station is the highest in the British Isles. As one waits for a train in the morning, the only sound is the *go-back, go-back* of grouse sounding off like alarm clocks in the heathery wastes round about. In the station-master's office three teapots stand cheerfully on top of a stove full of blazing coal, and every now and then there comes a tinkle or clonk from the massive lumps of Victorian safety equipment, still in daily use, which govern the passage of trains up and down the single line by means of heavy metal tokens or keys handed out to passing drivers.*

Only a few hardened hikers get on or off the train here, and the station would have closed long ago but for a quirk of history. When the West Highland Railway Company applied for permission to put the line through Corrour Forest in 1894, the laird, Sir John Stirling-Maxwell, agreed on one condition: that as long as his family remained in possession of the estate, the railway would furnish a halt at which guests might join or leave the train.

In those days a pony and trap met one at the railway and drove the short distance to the western end of Loch Ossian, where a steam launch sat ready to proceed in state to the lodge. Now one has to bounce along a rough road that skirts the loch-side; but at least the present laird is a grandson of Sir John, and British Rail, honouring its agreement, has kept the station open.

---

* Alas, these have at last given way to electronic controls.

Rescue of a fallen Dutchman*

We heard the first faint cries at six on Tuesday morning, but they came so dimly through the roar of the burn that we thought they were the bleating of sheep. It took the experienced ear of Tim Healy, head stalker on the Glenkinglass estate, to recognize the noise as the shout of a human in distress.

At 9 am, spying the mountain opposite the lodge through binoculars, we spotted a man waving a red garment, propped up against a big stone on the lip of the Raven's Burn, 1,000 feet above us and a mile away.

At once Tim set off up the hill with his young assistant, sixteen-year-old Alistair Loder. Through binoculars we eventually saw them reach the man. A few seconds later, a flare soared out. We took off with an emergency kit of stretcher, ropes and blankets.

Twenty minutes later, sweating and gasping, we found that the casualty – a thirty-two-year-old Dutch maths teacher, Ton (short for Antonius) Peters – had broken his left leg. He was grey in the face, shuddering and intermittently speechless with pain. As soon as we saw him, we decided he was too badly hurt for us to move him, so Tim went racing back down the mountain and set out on the fifty-minute drive to the nearest telephone to call in a helicopter.

Up on the mountain, we soon found that an epic feat of will-power and endurance had been performed. Eased by a pain-killing tablet, changed into a dry jersey, and wrapped in blankets, Peters was able to recount his ordeal.

An experienced hill walker and marathon runner, he was on a solitary trek that would have taken him from Glasgow to Glencoe. At about 3.30 pm on Friday he tried to cross the Raven's Burn, but missed his footing and fell thirty feet into the narrow ravine. At once he knew he was in severe trouble, for his left thigh was broken high up, and he could see the end of the bone pushing out against the muscles. Yet, far from panicking, he made a definite plan. 'I thought of what an animal does when it is injured,' he said. 'For the first couple of days it lies up, gaining strength, and then gradually it gets moving again. I hoped I could do the same. I thought that after a

---

* This article appeared in the *Sunday Telegraph* in 1984 and is reprinted by kind permission of the Editor of that newspaper. I wanted to include it in this collection to commemorate the great fortitude of Ton.

136

couple of days the bone would start to knit, and I would be able to climb out of the ravine.'

Having dragged himself out of the pool into which he had fallen, he set up a makeshift camp on a flat slab of rock at the foot of two waterfalls – and there he spent the next three days. Lying on his back on a mat, with his sleeping-bag and tent spread over him, he was warm and relatively comfortable. He had plenty of food, and brewed up several meals on his gas cooker: soup, savoury rice, tea and cereal. Occasional aspirin helped dull the pain and enabled him to sleep for short stretches. He had four pain-killing tablets, but preserved them against the ordeal of trying to climb out of the ravine.

Whenever he thought he heard any sound that could have been made by humans, he shouted for help, but the gorge was so narrow that his voice did not carry far. After a while he began to suffer mild hallucinations, and at one stage heard his mother talking to him. To help time pass he kept a diary, writing neatly in a small notebook.

Saturday and Sunday were mercifully fine and warm. But on Monday afternoon it began to rain, gently at first, then harder. At 7 pm there was a cloudburst high up the mountain. Twenty minutes later a surge of white water came roaring down the burn channel and shattered Peters's camp.

His equipment went first: tent, sleeping-bag and pack were swept away. Then he himself was lifted bodily and thrown down the ravine. How far he went, neither he nor we could tell, but it was at least 150 yards and over several waterfalls.

When at last he fetched up against a fallen tree trunk, he could feel that his left leg had been smashed up much worse than before. Nevertheless, he had to get out of the raging torrent or drown. So, by a superhuman effort, he fought his way up an almost vertical, fifteen-foot rockface, and then up a very steep bank of grass and heather.

The ground he had crossed was scrabbled black, as if a badger had been caught in a snare. It took him four hours to reach the lip of the ravine. From there he could see straight down to our lodge but, as he watched, the lights went out and he was left to spend his fourth night in the open, now clad only in shorts, shirt and jersey – all sodden.

All this he recounted, in perfect English, as we waited for the helicopter. He was amazingly cheerful, worried only about his chances of being able to run again. A search of the ravine below where he had finished up yielded his sleeping-bag and pack, both badly torn.

His equipment, otherwise excellent, had one vital deficiency: he carried no whistle. If he had had one, he would have attracted our attention far sooner. He had known this, and as he progressed through the Highlands he had repeated tried to buy a whistle, without success.

It was a 1,000-to-one fluke that we found him at all. Glenkinglass Lodge is the only house within a seven-mile radius of where he was hurt. If he had fallen into any other ravine, the chances are that nothing would have been found but his bones.

At last a Royal Navy Sea King helicopter came skimming up the glen. The slope was too steep for it to land, so it hovered twenty feet above the heather while two crewmen and a civilian doctor came down on the winches. Quickly they gave Peters a sedative jab, sheathed his leg in a pneumatic splint, lashed him into the stretcher and hoisted him aloft.

Thanks to the professional skill of the crew, the rescue itself was straightforward, but as the helicopter lifted away over the ridges to the south and silence returned to the glen, we realized that we had witnessed a miracle of courage and survival.

Mystery of the buried eggs

As I swung into the farmyard the other evening I caught a fox full in the headlights, outside the old stable door. Whipping round, it went over the garden wall like a ghostly russet streak and disappeared into the night, but its presence in the homestead, only an hour after dark, suddenly suggested a clue to the Mystery of the Buried Eggs.

This has had us baffled for some time. Every now and then we dig up a fresh chicken's egg in the vegetable patch. How did it get there – inside a wire-netting fence, fifty yards from the nest in the straw bales?

At first I thought the thief must be a rat. Then I considered a hedgehog, which I had seen about the yard and which, if it breathed in hard, could just about squeeze itself under the garden gate. Yet the distance which the eggs had travelled seemed beyond the normal scope of either creature and suggested some longer-legged transporter.

A badger, then? No – because Brock, if he wanted to enter the garden, would force his way under the wire and leave a telltale hole. Now that I have caught the fox almost, but not quite, *in flagrante delicto,* a few feet from the nest, I am inclined to believe that he is the culprit. Even so, I cannot quite see why he wants to bury eggs among the potatoes, unless it is out of thrift against lean times later in the year.

One way of solving the puzzle would be to load an egg with a bleeper, which would sound an alarm in the house if it was shifted. Then, if it started to move off during the hours of darkness, I could sally forth with a torch and see what is really happening. But I am inclined to think that it is hardly worth the bother and that, in any case, I would rather preserve an element of mystery about what goes on in the still watches.

The Drooper strikes back

This being the season of mellow fruitfulness, it is perhaps in order to sing the praises of that stalwart member of our establishment, the Warwickshire Drooper. Let no one think this a smutty reference to some ancient retainer who is getting past it: fruit growers will straightaway recognize the Drooper as a species of plum tree.

Ours grew hard by the back door and, when, on taking over the house two years ago, we decided to make a terrace there, it had to go. Since it was only about six feet tall, one scoop from the digger was enough to exhume it bodily, and at my behest the driver dumped it out in the paddock.

There it lay for the whole of the winter. Its roots were fairly well protected from frost by a ball of earth, but the horses ate off most of its outer branches, and the more I looked at its tattered remains, the more I feared I should have to burn them.

In April, however, I pulled myself together, dragged the tree into the tractor bucket, brought it down into the orchard, dug a large hole, rolled it in, gave it a lavish dose of manure, watered it and hoped for the best. That summer it rallied feebly and put out about half a dozen plums, which experts diagnosed as its final fling before expiring.

This year it has confounded us all. First it was a mass of blossom, then a riot of fruit. To celebrate its recovery, I decided to count the plums, but gave up when I passed 300. It may easily have borne 1,000, smaller than Victorias, but passing sweet. This has, I know, been an exceptional year for plums, but I would willingly back the Drooper against all comers in any contest for the title of Tree that Came Back from the Dead.

Whether or not its performance heralds a hard winter, it would be rash to prophesy; but hazel nuts and hawthorn berries are also super-abundant, and already people in the village are beginning to reminisce cosily about the last great freeze, when our lane was blocked for a month and the drifts in town were so deep that the Council's snow-ploughs kept finding they had Minis in their buckets when they went to dig out the streets.

** The signs were confounded and the winter turned out exceptionally mild.

Fruits of the season

At this time of the year it is hard to escape Taffy, most regular of regulars at the Lamb Inn, enunciating with terrific emphasis his theory of blackberry picking: for every berry gathered, he claims, thousands go to waste. From this it follows that it is 'bloody ridiculous' for any landowner to resent pickers invading his territory.

The first part of Taffy's Law may well be correct. Nevertheless, I find it hard to remain entirely calm when I see ladies from the village advancing, baskets in hand, towards my modest preserves. I can spot them a mile off, for their gait is quite different from that of ordinary walkers: like hens, they peck their way along the hedges and, once they reach a fruitful area, start sidling crabwise.

Now it so happens that the best blackberries in the vicinity grow along a fence between two of my fields. Because the site lies in full view of our windows and is not on a footpath, strangers need some nerve to tackle it, but tackle it they do, and I cannot help plotting schemes of deterrence.

A couple of rounds from a full-bore rifle into the bank above would certainly be effective, but rather unkind. Better to use subtler methods: a notice saying 'Beware of the Bull', or a sign warning of adders. But of course the ultimate deterrent is to get out there at crack of dawn myself and pick all the ripe blackberries, wishing Taffy to the devil as I do so.

The question of what one may or may not legitimately pick up for oneself in woods and fields is hard to answer. Wild fruits like blackberries, crab apples, sloes, hazel nuts and mushrooms are obviously fair game (of game itself – pheasants and partridges – I do not speak here, for that is another subject); but what if I come on apples in the orchard of a house that has been deserted? Clearly the property belongs to somebody, but there is no one here now and, if I do not scrump a few of the apples, they are going to be wasted . . .

It seems to me that in every true countryman there lurks a bit of a scrounger. The attitude comes directly from wild creatures, birds particularly, which wake up every morning with nothing, and have to go out and find their daily sustenance. Countrymen share this opportunistic outlook: if they see a trifle lying unconsidered in field or hedgerow, their natural inclination is to pick it up.

Besides, any such tendency is of course increased by neglect or bad management. On a well-run farm, where everything is ship-shape, you have the feeling that somebody knows what point every project has reached and that any interference will at once be detected. But on badly run estates, where trees that fall down are not cleared up and equipment is left lying about, you can be sure that no one will notice if you carry off the odd lump of firewood . . . and so on.

My biggest ever windfall was a buck rake (which fits on to the back of a tractor). This belonged to a notoriously careless forestry contractor, who had already strewn several other pieces of equipment about the woods, among them a capacious trailer which was in a state of some decay but nevertheless excited our cupidity.

We spotted the buck rake under a heap of brushwood and kept watch on it from one season to the next. When, after five winters, it had not once moved, we dragged it out, took it to the farm, cleaned it up and started to use it. I am sorry to say that we also did a little to disguise it by scraping off the remains of its blue paint.

If its owner turned up and claimed it, we told ourselves, we would just hand it back and thank him for the loan. But although he was often about the estate, he never said a word. Far from feeling contrite, we were only sorry that we had not had the nerve to appropriate the trailer as well, for this, though still *in situ*, was by then a ruin.

Taking a jaundiced view

I suppose it is foolish to worry about the colour of one's boots. Black or brown or green – what does it matter? Provided they are comfortable and strong, that should be enough. All the same, I could not help feeling dismayed when a new and expensive pair of walking-boots that I had ordered by post emerged from their wrappings the colour of ripe bananas.

My first reaction was to send them straight back. Nothing, I thought, would induce me to wear anything so ridiculous. I felt I had been conned: the advertisement which caught my eye should have declared that the goods on offer bore so fearfully jaundiced an appearance.

My irritation was sharpened by a cocky message on the sales tag boasting that the leather had been treated with some special process which rendered further dressing unnecessary. This suggested that the violent yellow would never tone down: once a banana, always a banana.

Mastering my distaste, I put the boots on and crept out for a walk, slinking furtively uphill and into the wood along a path very little frequented. My worst fears were confirmed: water rolled off the patent dressing as off a duck, and I returned with my feet every bit as luminous as at the outset.

After a week of having to stand rooted in long grass or nettles whenever another pedestrian approached, I decided on desperate measures. First I heated some leather-oil to almost boiling point, then applied it freely. The effect was miraculous: at a stroke the boots went from banana to coffee. A second coat turned them chocolate, and now, 100 miles and ten further doses later, they are the colour of old chestnuts, besides fitting perfectly. But had I not ignored the manufacturers' self-satisfied instructions, I might well have thrown £75 away in disgust.

Invasion of the homestead

The first hint of trouble came when the telephone rang at 9.10 pm, just as we were finishing supper. The caller was my in-laws' neighbour,

143

who lives at the bottom of the lane leading up to their isolated farm-house. The publican across the green had told him that streams of rough-looking bikers were coming in to buy vodka and asking for directions to the house. Did I know where my in-laws were?

'No,' I told him, 'but I'll soon find out.'

Three telephone calls ran them to earth at a weekend retreat in Wales. Was there *supposed* to be a party going on in their house?

'No!' they cried – and then, 'God, it must be Sheila, the new nanny.'

'I'm going over,' I told them. 'Call the police.'

Sheila, a local girl, had not even been left in charge of the cottage: it had merely been arranged that she should go up to check the animals. I drove like Jehu. For Ramoth Gilead read Stokenchurch, through which I passed at ninety miles an hour. As I bounced up the track to the little house, I saw that the place was lit up like Blackpool. Music was blasting out. The yard was bristling with bikes.

My immediate instinct was to barricade in all these people, whoever they were, so that they should not escape justice. I therefore parked diagonally between the high hedges, blocking the road, and locked the car.

Primed by alarm and anger, I rushed straight in. The dining-room – no more than twelve feet square – was packed with people, roaring with noise, dense with smoke. The smell of alcohol and glue was overpowering. Instinctively I made for the stereo and pulled out the plug. Into the sudden silence I yelled, 'Get out, quick! The fuzz are coming.'

There was a moment's calm, then a roar of obscenities. Luckily I had had the forethought to put on a camouflaged combat-jacket, and this, reinforced by sheer rage, must have increased the impact of my sudden appearance. The revellers were unsettled. Most of them in any case looked only about fifteen.

'Where's Sheila?' I yelled. 'Get Sheila!'

Sheila was in an armchair, under four or five boys. They dug her out, but she was too far gone to make sense. Again I shouted, 'Everybody out!' People began to move. Through the French windows which gave on to the garden I saw the terrace come alive with sprinting figures.

I ran upstairs. My in-laws' double bed held three skinny couples. 'Out, the lot of you!' I roared. Back downstairs, I found I had been reinforced by Sheila's father, alerted by telephone from Wales. Then the police arrived, accelerating the mass departure; but the sergeant maintained there was not much he could do, since all the party-goers insisted that they had been invited.

With most of the bodies gone, an unspeakable mess stood revealed. The tiled floor in the dining-room was awash with drink, littered with beer cans, cigarette stubs, crisp packets, pieces of bread. Empty wine bottles lay everywhere. The first few I looked at had contained supermarket plonk, but then I found a couple of Wine Society claret, and my worst suspicions were confirmed when I came on a bottle of Château Latour 1964, with half an inch left in the bottom.

I grabbed the sergeant, who was about to leave, and pointed out that the alleged guests had broken into my brother-in-law's wine. Still he said that no charges could be brought. I called Wales. 'I'm here,' I said. 'There *has* been a party, but it's broken up ... Yes, about eighty people.'

'Eighty! We'll come straight back.'

'No, no!' Seeing the state of the place, and knowing the impact it would have if they arrived at 2 am, after a three-hour drive, I positively forbade them to return until morning. Instead, they eased their feelings by firing Sheila there and then, over the telephone, and telling her to get out, with all her belongings, inside an hour.

By midnight she had sobered up enough for some inkling of her unpopularity to sink through. Her boyfriend, whom I would have called a bare-faced liar had his cheeks not been covered with sup-purating spots, brazenly insisted to the last that everyone had gate-crashed. Even when I showed him one of Sheila's hand-written invitations, which I had found on the floor, advertising that the party would be 'from seven till late!', he dismissed it as a forgery.

They left with her in tears. Her father, who had been heroic at clearing up in humiliating circumstances, took them off. I then found that my own car had been bundled into the hedge, stripped of windscreen wipers, radio aerial and mirrors, and well scratched all over.

A few frustrated revellers were still circling the place at a distance, hooting like Red Indians in the woods. I therefore rang Wales once more and said that I intended to spend the rest of the night *in situ*. The house, though by then tidy, stank like a pub at closing time.

Eventually, at about 2 am, I went to bed, but I hardly slept at all, for at first light a bantam cock began to crow and my dogs, taking it for an intruder, gave it how-de-do every time it uttered. Driven up again soon after six, I searched the garden and was rewarded by the discovery of several bottles thrown away unopened as panic set in. Among them was one of Château Latour, standing on its head in the roses.

Sheila later confessed that she *had* organized the party, the nucleus being a gang of bikers whom she had met on holiday. Under pressure from her father, she agreed to repay by small instalments as much as she could of the expense incurred, which included £500 for repairs to my car.

Afterwards several people remarked on how brave I had been to wade into a scene of that kind. At the time it never occurred to me that there was any risk – and I am sure I was helped by the fact that I felt so angry, which communicated itself powerfully. What would have happened if I had *not* arrived, I cannot say, but it was clear that the party had been growing wilder by the minute and the whole place could easily have been burned down. The moral seems to be that it is unwise to leave a tucked-away country house empty, with a teenager whom you scarcely know able to gain access.

Country cooking secrets

What the eye does not see... The other evening I had occasion to deliver some meat to the landlord of a country pub whose restaurant has an excellent reputation in the neighbourhood. The car-park was packed, and dinner was already in full swing. As I stood in the scullery, waiting for mine host to return with some money, the chef (whom I might, if I were feeling uncharitable, describe as a yobbo) rushed in exclaiming, 'Christ! *Another* order for lamb chops *chasseur!*'

Diving into the deep-freeze, he came up with a stick of four or five chops joined together. This he promptly dumped in the sink, forcing it down among a mass of dirty plates and cutlery. He then turned the hot tap on it and rushed off to attend to his next culinary masterpiece.

Now it may well be that by the time the chops reached the unsuspecting diner's table, they looked and tasted marvellous, untainted by the faintest trace of washing-up liquid or other people's leftovers. But in that moment of disillusionment I for one took an instant vow that I would never eat in that pub again.

Waste not...

'Place like this, you should never throw anything away,' said our builder as we rootled around the farmyard for a piece of slate to use in recapping a chimney.

'Well,' I began cautiously (for I had already had one gigantic clear-out and was planning another), 'a lot of this stuff is rubbish...'

'Never!' he said. 'Might come in handy any time.' And then he settled the point with an unanswerable observation: 'I mean, stood in a corner there, it don't eat nor drink nothing, do it?'

The egg thief exposed

When I described, a little earlier, how fresh chicken's eggs kept appearing mysteriously among our potatoes, dug well into the soil, I got a blast of scepticism for suggesting that the nocturnal transporter must be a fox. People have been assuring me that the thief is a hedgehog, but an altogether more mischievous suggestion was put forward by Mr Pierce Power of Orford, in Cheshire.

Mr Power maintained that the planting of an egg among the vegetables used to be much favoured in Ireland as a means of blighting your neighbour's crops. Well, it may be that I have a neighbour so ill-disposed as to come sparring about the farmyard and garden at midnight, but all I can say is that, if I do, his or her ministrations have so far proved spectacularly unsuccessful.

It could, of course, have been an egg that did for the courgettes, whose stalks rotted in the wet; yet, apart from them, our vegetables have been stupendous. I do not aim to grow the kind of monsters which carry off prizes at the local agricultural show – onions the size of footballs strike me as vaguely obscene – and I use no artificial fertilizer, but it has to be admitted that our winter spinach has reached a size that can only be described as ridiculous, and you could easily mistake my broccoli patch for a stretch of tropical rainforest.

In other words, I do not buy Mr Power's idea – and now in any case support for my own theory is rolling in. From another reader, near Bath, comes news of a vixen which appears every evening, sometimes in the dusk but often in full daylight, in search of scraps.

The animal has grown so bold that she sits in the vegetable patch, looking in through the kitchen window to assess her chances of a meal. The owners of the house, who supply her lavishly, had for some time suspected her of burying food, and recently she settled their doubts by allowing one of them to approach within six feet of her while she dug a hole, put a small piece of chicken in it, and *covered it with her nose.*

If final proof were needed, I find it in a new book, *Running with the Fox*, by that great expert and enthusiast David Macdonald. In this the author describes how an infant, hand-reared vixen called Niff became 'a compulsive maker of caches' while still a cub, hiding pieces of food indoors beneath any object she could find, such as his notebooks or even his pillows, which she invariably pushed into place on top of the hoard with her nose.

Later she grew up to become the first of twenty foxes with whom he had 'a thrilling professional relationship' – they the instructors, he the student – and she taught him an immense amount about vulpine behaviour. One of his most fascinating discoveries was that foxes make literally dozens of food caches during their nocturnal prowls and that, although their powers of navigating back to their own little hoards are phenomenal, one animal cannot usually detect the buried treasure of another.

Night warfare in the woods

With the leaves beginning to fall – and night visibility therefore opening up in the woods – pheasant poachers are once again going into top gear for their short but lucrative season. For anyone engaged in protecting an estate against invaders, nocturnal skirmishes are exciting and enjoyable; but they are also dangerous, for if a clash occurs the aim on both sides is to give the opposition what is known locally as 'a bloody good hiding' and answer questions (if any) afterwards.

For years we have been mildly annoyed by a man in the village who is so brazen that, come November, he openly takes orders in the pub for pheasants, which he guarantees to supply in time for Christmas. He is a nuisance, certainly, but only a moderate one. A far greater menace are the gangs who come in by car from some distance away, three or four strong, armed with powerful air-rifles or silenced .22s. If a party of this kind gets loose in a prime covert on a windy night (when the noise of shots is swept away), they can inflict substantial damage.

Of course we have key rides and tracks wired up with alarm-guns, but by far the best deterrent against such raiders is an Alsatian. If poachers hear that a big dog is on patrol in the woods of a particular estate, they tend to seek their fortune elsewhere, for they know that in an encounter the dog can easily outrun them and will infallibly sniff them out if they seek to hide.

Alarm bells therefore rang instantly when, at 9 pm one night last year, the gamekeeper telephoned to announce that Tammy, his Alsatian bitch, had been kidnapped. This dog, which always reacted ferociously to the approach of a stranger, could not have been got out of her kennel without a violent struggle unless she had been doped. Someone must have crept up to the isolated cottage in the dark, tossed her a piece of baited meat, waited a few minutes and lugged her away.

Clearly some major operation was about to be launched. Pausing only to fill a flask with coffee, we went out in the Land Rover, and we did not return until the sky was starting to lighten eight hours later. All night we dodged from one wood to another, driving without lights across the frozen fields, lurking, waiting, moving on quickly, going back on our tracks, occasionally shouting, flashing a torch abruptly.

How many of them there were, how close we came to them, we never knew. But that they were on the ground was certain, for at 3.45 am a vehicle came cruising through the private road with no lights on, and accelerated away when we suddenly fell in behind it. As dawn began to break, we could see black lumps of pheasants still roosting safely in the trees and knew that we had won the war of nerves for one night anyway.

And Tammy? She limped home at nine in the morning. When she came round – perhaps in a van or in a strange house – she cannot have been an attractive proposition, and we presumed that her captors had simply turned her loose. For us humans, and I daresay for her too, it had been a night to remember.

Magic of the rut

In woods frequented by fallow deer, the next few days will usher in the climax of the year, for the annual rut is now building to its peak. The deer are in a state of intense excitement, which communicates itself to any human fortunate enough to witness their manoeuvres. Since these are mainly nocturnal or crepuscular, watching them is not easy; but even in the dark it is simple enough to locate a rutting-stand, for every master buck, once he had taken up his territory, proclaims his presence by continuous calling.

At this time of year many an urban walker returns from a stroll looking pale and declaring that he has just heard 'a bloody great pig' grunting down in the wood. In fact what he has heard is a fallow buck groaning, a kind of heavyweight snorting, harsh and abrupt at close quarters.

Once established on his stand, the buck parades up and down advertising his presence not merely by his voice, but also by his smell, which by now has become formidable, freshened up by his habit of rolling in his own urine. All round – skittering about in anticipation, chivvied up and down – flit such does as he has been able to wrest from rivals. It is the females who have set this whole process in train by starting to come into season; but now that their hour is at hand, they are incredibly reluctant to submit to the male's advances.

I once saw a sex-crazed buck pursue a doe clean out of the wood, down some fields, up a valley, back into the trees – at least a mile, all at full gallop – and still she would not stand for him. The result is that the master bucks end up utterly exhausted.

On the stand itself, behind the does, in an outer orbit, circle lesser bucks who are trying to get in on the action. This offers the stalker a rare chance to cull old or sub-standard beasts, for seasoned gentlemen never seen during the rest of the year (which they spend in some tucked-away cervine equivalent of Boodle's or White's) now venture out into the open, drawn by the irresistible prospect of procreation.

The most stirring spectacle of all is that of a fight. Combat is usually preceded by a short ritual progress, in which two bucks walk parallel, shoulder to shoulder, haunch to haunch, as though unaware of each other. Far from it: suddenly in unison they wheel inwards, clash antlers and wrestle for supremacy, often with such violence that they go hurtling sideways through patches of undergrowth, causing tremendous noise and a further increase in all-round tension. Most fights are inconclusive, with the weaker animal retiring for the time being; but sometimes, if a buck's brow-tines penetrate an opponent's ribs, a battle can end in death.

For me, the magic of the rut lies partly in the fact that it takes place in lovely surroundings: I know of no better time than daybreak in the woods on a frosty October morning. Yet still more haunting is the knowledge that one is witnessing an age-old ritual – an event that has taken place not for a hundred autumns or even for a thousand, but for tens of thousands, and feels nearly as ancient as the earth itself.

Reading telltale signs

The longer a person spends in the woods, the more skilful he or she becomes at interpreting the signs left by other creatures. Gamekeepers, in particular, grow extraordinarily adept at reading small traces: a footprint in the mud of the gateway, a twig broken beside the ride, grass flattened, feathers on the plough, a strand of wool on barbed wire. Often from such trifles a whole scenario can be deduced.

Nevertheless, mysteries remain. Earlier this week, for instance, I shot a fallow buck which turned out to have a small, triangular patch of purple dye on its chest. The colour was exactly that of the antibiotic spray now widely used by vets and farmers. But how had this wild animal come to be marked? Nobody can explain.

Still less explicable was the pair of trousers which I once found, deep in a wood, knotted round the branch of a rhododendron bush. The legs had been tied together six or eight times, the knots drawn tight with such maniacal strength that only a knife would release them.

What could have driven the owner to divest himself of his nether garment and leave it thus exhibited? As we speculated, my companion and I remarked to ourselves that if the conformation of the man's legs in any way resembled that of his trousers, his gait must be striking, to say the least.

Inedible corn on the cob

Many of the farmers who grow maize for silage are finding this year's crop exceptionally good. The corn really has climbed as high as an elephant's eye – eight or nine feet, instead of the usual seven – and, although it has ripened late, it is now yielding a bumper harvest.

Anyone living near a field and seeing cobs by the thousand must feel tempted to sneak home a couple for the table. If they do, I guarantee they will try it once only, because the strains of maize developed for agriculture, although palatable to cattle when chopped up by a forage harvester, do not lend themselves to cooking. The cobs may *look* beautifully succulent and even, but when boiled or steamed the grains of corn go hard as bullets.

Having found this out by painful experience, I am tantalized by a recurrent fantasy. In this I slip out into a field at dusk, cut several thousand cobs, pile them into a van with false number plates, drive overnight to London, and at dawn unload on to unsuspecting traders at the new Covent Garden market. Because I am not a regular supplier, the price obviously has to be rather low. Nevertheless, I abscond with a substantial sum in cash.

The question is, how long would it be before consumers, dentures and digestion shattered, started to bombard the market with recriminations? My hunch is that very few people would ever complain: most would think that the ruination of the corn was somehow their own fault and would lie low rather than risk making fools of themselves. All the same, I fancy it is a trick that I should not try to pull more than once.

When is a shrike not a shrike?

Each morning, from the field of a neighbour, comes a sound that brings back a painful but salutary episode from my childhood.

Every now and then a roguish but agreeable character called Jack Cook, ruddy of cheek and mobile of eyebrow, used to turn up for a day's ferreting or pigeon shooting with the gamekeeper, in whose company I spent every possible minute of my school holidays.

Jack used to address me as 'Buoy', elongating the word with

deliberately artificial rusticity, as though it referred to yachting. One day, aged eleven, I told him I had heard a peculiar noise in the wood beneath our house.

'Ah!' he said instantly. 'That's a red-backed shrike. Rare old bird, that. You want to get down there arter 'ee.' He went on to describe a bird that looked something like a jay – reddish-brown and blue on the back, pinkish on the breast, with a black and white tail – which catches smaller birds and impales them on thorns.

Eagerly I looked up the shrike in my book. There it was, exactly as Jack had said, known from its carnivorous habits as 'the butcher bird'. Somehow I must have missed or misinterpreted the line which gave its voice as 'few shrill notes in May and June'. The sound I was pursuing could not conceivably have been described as that. All the same, hearing the call, I often rushed down the wood full of expectation, but the giver of it always eluded me.

'Seen that there bird yet, Buoy?' Jack would ask every time he met me; and when I confessed failure, he gave me to understand that I would never make a countryman if I did not set eyes on a red-backed shrike. I began to feel inadequate.

How long the game lasted, and how it was finally blown, I cannot remember. Eventually I somehow discovered that the phantom cries were coming not from the wood but from a field beyond, and were made not by a shrike, but by a donkey.

Jack was delighted, of course, that I had taken so long to rumble him. I was humiliated by the exposure of my ignorance. But now, as our donkey Snowball lets rip, squeaking and roaring every day at mid-morning, I look back almost with satisfaction, feeling that to have had my leg well pulled at such a formative age did me no end of good.

New use for a hot potato

Walking home earlier this week, I came on a car wedged securely across the lane, tail in one high bank, bonnet in the other. The lady driver, emerging at a reckless speed (in reverse) from the track that goes up at an angle to the church, had both got herself stuck and stalled her engine.

'It's extraordinary,' she said as I approached, 'normally it starts at a touch, but now it won't go at all.'

I saw at once what had happened: the car's exhaust pipe had been rammed into the bank and packed with earth. To free it was no easy matter, for before I could get at the obstruction I had to heave and jerk the vehicle round far enough to gain access to the end of the pipe. But then, by poking with a stick, I was able to break up the block in a few seconds; the engine started with a healthy roar, blowing out the loosened crumbs of soil.

The driver was amazed that I had diagnosed her problem so quickly. Little did she know that I had had experience in this very field – for the deliberate blocking of an exhaust pipe is much favoured by gamekeepers as a means of immobilizing vehicles found parked in suspicious circumstances at night. A clod of earth or mud will do the trick, but still better is a large potato, tapped onto the pipe so that a core is cut out and the outside part can be pulled off and thrown away. (The exhaust must have had time to cool down; if it is hot, the block will shrink and probably become loose enough to be blown clear.)

A well-rammed potato will cause dire problems, as it is almost impossible to detect in the dark, and even harder to remove. The odds are that a poacher will simply sit there mystified, as the forces of law and order close in on him, running down his battery with the starter and wondering why in hell his engine will not fire.

On your marks, get set, BANG

Never mind that this year (1987) the first of November falls on a Sunday: at first light tomorrow morning the shooting men of Ireland, north and south, will be out in force for the opening of the pheasant season. No use to wait until the gentlemanly hour of nine or so: if you want to be in with a chance, you too will have to be on the ground before dawn breaks.

Although in Ireland shooting rights theoretically belong to the landowner or his assigns, in practice – as with so much else in the Emerald Isle – the rules are no more than a guide to what goes on. Thus, although some territory is energetically preserved and defended by signs warning off unauthorized persons, a great deal more ground is regarded as free for all.

Competition is intense in any area known to hold game – and for tomorrow morning much careful reconnaissance has already been put in: growing broods of pheasants have been marked down, plans laid, ambush positions selected, approach routes worked out. As the light comes up, a phenomenal bombardment will erupt from every quarter of the compass – and it will continue until, by the middle of

156

the morning, all the less wary birds are in the bag, and the wilier survivors have retired to unapproachable fastnesses in the bog.

The convention is that one shoots cock pheasants only and leaves the hens to breed. Yet on the first day of the season temptation is often too great – and excuses are easy enough. 'And didn't the poor creature have to fly straight out of the sun at me!' says the innocent slayer of a hen. 'Sure I never spotted her colour at all.'

So ubiquitous are the gunmen, so quick on the trigger, that sensible men call off their normal country pursuits for the day and stay at home. Thus, in Co. Tipperary, Donald Swan, master of the Golden Vale hunt (which in typical Irish fashion goes out on Sundays only), has cancelled the meet scheduled for tomorrow. Things tend to be even more dangerous in the north, for there terrorists may easily take advantage of the general bombardment to open up on targets larger than pheasants.

When I lived in Co. Tipperary, I had (on paper) exclusive rights to shoot on the land belonging to the house we rented; but often, as I worked my dog along an overgrown hedge in the hope of surprising a cock pheasant, I would become aware of unofficial opposition working the same hedge from the opposite direction. Sometimes a shot would go off a few hundred yards ahead: on other occasions a spaniel or terrier would suddenly emerge from the undergrowth close at hand and one or other of us would sheer off to avoid a confrontation.

The keenest shooting man in our area – and a formidable destroyer of vermin – was the Anglican canon, who was introduced to me as a 'fierce hard man at the duck' (only, this being Tipperary, the description came out as 'a fierce haird man at the dock'). This divine saw no harm at all in shooting on the Sabbath – and indeed it was during one of his high-speed dashes between the four parishes to which he ministered that his passion for vermin control led to a regrettable accident.

On a Sunday morning in November, as he hurtled from one service to the next, he suddenly clapped on his brakes with such violence that a car which he had just overtaken piled into him from behind, wrecking both vehicles and injuring the other driver. The reason for the canon's emergency stop? Through a gateway he had spotted a magpie, and he was reaching for the 12-bore which he carried ready on the back seat to open up on the hapless bird.

Reflections on moving house

We moved house a year ago yesterday and, although we are now well settled in our new environment, I still look back on our migration westwards as a traumatic event. Reflecting on it, I would pass over the mundane business of packing up our household effects, and concentrate on outdoor matters, were it not for my glowing memories of Tom, the leader of our removal gang.

'No problem!' was Tom's watchword – and be the tasks with which I confronted him never so ghastly, he solved every one by a combination of dexterity and sheer strength. Yet almost more valuable was his psychological support. Having moved countless other people, and seeing that we were in a state of shock, he went out of his way to soothe us with amusing stories. Several turned on the fact that pieces of furniture look quite different when taken out of their normal context:

'What on earth's that?' said the lady.

'It's your settee, Madam.'

'Nonsense!' she said. 'I've never seen it in my life. Take the horrible thing away.'

'Madam – it came from behind the door in your parlour...'

The best anecdote, however, was about the van full of eyes:

'We go to move this woman. "I've got some cats," she says.

'"Cats, madam. No problem. How many cats is it?"

'"A hundred and fifty cats."

'"A hundred and fifty cats. And where are they?"

'"In the lounge."

'"No problem, madam. I'll call in the RSPCA."

'Phone the RSPCA. Bloke turns up with a heap of wire cages. The smell in the lounge – you can't imagine it. Nearly killed us. Still, we load the cats, and away to the new location. Park by the kerb in a village. Start unloading – the van's back doors are open. Dark already, mind you. Suddenly there's this terrific screech of brakes. A man's drawn up behind the van. Leaps out of his car, comes dashing into the house. Obvious he's had a few.

'"Christ almighty!" he shouts. "What is it? What is it?"

'"What's what?" I ask.

'"Bloody eyes! There's hundreds of green eyes in that van. All moving!"

'"Relax," I tell him. "It's only some cats."

158

"'Ah, thank God," he says – and away he goes quite happy.'

Tom was terrific. He could easily have handled all our possessions, but we, hoping to save money, had elected to transport various outside effects ourselves.

Thus we found ourselves toiling back and forth, eighty miles in each direction, jeep and horse-box loaded with dog kennels, chicken coops, feed bins, troughs, spare timber, firewood, beanpoles, bicycles, gardening equipment and furniture, wheelbarrows, beehives (inhabited), ladders, toboggans, rainwater butts and – very handy, this, when you already have too much to carry – a small pony trap.

There was one job which I kept putting off: the recovery of our weather-vane, which was mounted dangerously high, some forty feet up on the roof of the barn. But then came a minor miracle.

For two days a westerly gale had been blowing and at teatime on the last afternoon the weather-vane took matters into its own hands, suddenly breaking loose from its anchorage, rolling down the roof, and landing undamaged at my feet – the clearest possible signal to depart.

By eight o'clock I was forty miles out on my final run, with four peacocks, ten chickens and one dog on board, when I realized that I had left behind the key of the new house. The result was that I had to press one of the ladders into service immediately I arrived and force an entry head first through the top half of the bathroom window.

It has taken time to evaluate the differences between our old and new environments: fresh ones keep emerging.

One of the most welcome is in the texture of the soil; instead of flints and chalk, we have rich deep loam the colour of milk chocolate. This makes gardening a delight and greatly eases the labour of tasks like driving in fence-posts or planting trees.

As before, we are surrounded by woods and hills, but the nature of both is different. The hills are steeper, the valleys deeper; the woods have (to me) an alien mix of trees – more ash and sycamore, less beech and fir.

Most houses are of stone, rather than brick and flint; stone walls bound many of the fields, and the craft of dry-stone walling still flourishes. The balance of nature is different, too. No doubt it is the soft earth that encourages badgers, which are far more numerous here than there: well-trodden highways lead up and down the valley sides, and the woods are dotted with prodigious earthworks.

Foxes also abound, not least because we are on the boundary between two flourishing hunts, whose activities paradoxically increase the numbers of their quarry; and there are, in consequence, extraordinarily few rabbits.

Birds of prey seem to thrive – almost certainly because not much active gamekeeping goes on. Buzzards circle above the head of the valley, sparrowhawks skim the hedges, and at dusk the woods come alive with the screeching of little owls.

Good as it is to see so many predators, the profusion has its drawbacks. In the absence of vermin control, magpies and crows flourish. The result is that there are far fewer small birds (whose eggs are eaten by magpies) than I expected. Yet this again has one beneficial consequence: that it is possible to grow raspberries without a net or cage, as there are not enough blackbirds and thrushes to eat them.

A year ago I would never have believed it possible, but now I see that our few losses are easily outweighed by our gains. One is a real village shop, which doubles as a gossip centre; another is a local brewery which produces formidable old ale. But what greater gain could there be than to find oneself among people who are in so much less of a hurry that they always have time to stop and talk?

Judging solely by the map, we moved eighty miles farther from London, but in terms of civility and friendliness, we went back twenty years.

Up or down to London?

At supper the other night conversation turned on the question of whether one goes *up* or *down* to London. Most people held that it was simply of question of latitude: anyone living in the north (for instance, in Lancashire or Yorkshire) goes *down* to the capital, anyone in the south, like Kent or Sussex, *up*.

This seems sound as far as it goes. But it not entirely a question of where you are on the map. Why do we, who live level with London, still talk about going *up*? Is it because trains are still known as up-trains and down-trains? The answer, I believe, is that for us rustics the expression implies (correctly) that the city is a peak of artistic, intellectual and financial activity, to which one could not sensibly speak of descending.

Swedish bird in the hand

I was fascinated to find in the recently published diaries of the Norfolk gamekeeper, Larry Banville, a first-hand account of how he himself brought back the capercaillie to Scotland, where it had been extinct for seventy years.

The reintroduction of the caper from Scandinavia has long been one of the early success stories in conservation, but I have never seen it so well told. Now we have a vivid account of how Banville set off for Sweden in April 1837 at the behest of his employer, the Norfolk landowner T. F. Buxton, who wanted to repay hospitality he had enjoyed from Lord Breadalbane at Taymouth Castle, in Perthshire.

In Sweden, word had already gone out that capercaillie would be paid for, and a number of what Banville called 'the great birds' had been collected. In the end he assembled eleven cocks and fourteen hens, but he could not help being alarmed by the expense: 'Thursday 18 May. A fine cock bird came to us this day ... Its cost is now £5. What will it cost before it gets to the Highlands, if it ever do? This will cost T. F. Buxton Esquire £150 or £200 to do it well. What a lot of money to spend after the great birds.'

Thanks to Banville's vigilant management during the voyage, all except one of his charges reached Scotland safely, but at Taymouth Castle he was horrified to discover that no proper accommodation had been planned 'for my feathered family, who was under my care for so long a time'. He put the estate carpenters to work and soon was able to report that 'the house for the birds is getting on delightful'.

When the time came for him to leave and he was congratulated by the factor, he declared himself happy to have been 'the bearer of the birds to their native soil'. Now their descendants have spread to many a Highland glen and one feels he richly deserved the ovation which signalled his departure for the south: 'The servants of the castle – all sexes – gave me three times three to cheer poor Larry's heart.'

In Old Jasper's cider shed

You think you've tasted cider? Try this stuff, then, made beside the Severn by that master of the craft, Jasper Ely. 'If it's too tart for you, bloody hard luck,' he says. But it isn't too sharp by any means: compared with the sweet, fizzy, chemical liquid that you buy in shops, it is a celestial brew – alive, pungent, the essence of apples.

This being the cider-making season, we had gone in search of Old Jasper to glean some of his secrets. His smallholding is not – it must be said – a model of hygiene. Ramshackle farm buildings set in a sea of mud house a substantial population of pigs, principally Gloucester Old Spots, and out the back his fifteen-acre orchard of apples, pears and plums is tenanted by goats, donkeys, geese, turkeys and exotic breeds of poultry. But the hub of the establishment is the cider shed, presided over by Jasper himself, his face a striking shade of pink, his mane of snowy beard and whiskers topped by a tweed cap, his shirt wide open at the neck to reveal acres of tattoo on his chest. Once the stable of an inn, the shed is long, high, and narrow, of a Hogarthian dimness, with wooden casks ranged along one wall.

Jasper leans against a barrel, mug in hand. 'Anyone can make good cider, provided he can get good fruit,' he pronounces. 'There's absolutely nothing to it. Just smash up the apples, get the juice out of them and put it in a cask, and it starts to ferment on its own because the wild yeast is there present. Only don't kill it, that's all.

'Trouble is, nowadays, getting the damn fruit. Once upon a time there used to be orchards the whole way from here to Gloucester. This village *was* a bloody orchard, nothing else. Now most of the trees have been ripped out.

'What you've got to realize is that there are over 200 varieties of cider apple. Bulmer's Norman, Sweet Coppin, Sheepsnout, Yarlington Mill, Dabinett, Michelin ... a lot of the names are French. Bound to be, because cider come here with the Conqueror, didn't it?

'They're quite different from eating or cooking apples. Got more tannin in them. That's the keeping agent. Does the same job as hops in beer. If you use ordinary apples, you'll get *something*, but it won't be proper cider. Mind you, you can loose a few bags of summat else in the brew, and it'll be all right.'

In the murky air of the shed the smell is almost overpowering: effusions of apple and pig battle for supremacy, for although the

162

cider we are drinking is last year's, the first of this season's crop is coming in. The fruit is ground up in a crusher which stands in the open, between two pigsties. Each half-ton batch of pulp goes into a 100-gallon cask for twenty-four hours and then is loaded into ten nylon sacks, which are stacked one on top of another, like a huge sandwich, in the jaws of the press.

This vintage contraption, older than the century, is wound slowly down by hand through a series of worn gears, and even in bottom gear it is hard work to keep the flywheel going. Volunteers take turns. Down, down, down goes the plate, inexorably squeezing the sacks of pulp. Juice pours out into black plastic buckets. As each fills it is borne away and emptied into one of the storage casks.

'One thing we don't have to worry about is harvesting,' Jasper observes. 'Knock 'em off and that's near enough. But of course there's summers and summers. If you get bags of sunshine, you'll have a higher concentration of sugar in the fruit, and that'll mean more alcohol in the cider. *This* year, now, we didn't get much sun, but although we had a lot of wet days, we didn't get much rain either – so it won't be a great vintage.'

The number of people present seems to be growing. There is Jasper's assistant Pete, also lavishly bewhiskered and clad in yellow oilskins; two fair-haired teenagers; two or three unidentified persons . . . to say nothing of several dogs, which skid about on the film of juice and mud that covers the stone-flagged floor. Human conversation is backed by the constant trickle of juice and outbursts of chatter from the Old Spot sow and her thirteen piglets over the wall. She seems to know that she will be getting the mush or crushed fruit when it emerges from the press.

'Twenty-six year ago I come here,' Jasper is saying. 'I'd been to sea, been in the army, been a fishermen's bailiff, spent a bob, saved a bob. How did I get this place? *Bought* the bugger! They don't give 'em away, do they?'

Now sixty-one, he has lived on his own since his mother died. Has he never thought of getting married? 'You're joking! Give half your grub away to get the other half cooked? No bank manager'd give you a loan on that. Don't muck about, up there – keep winding!'

The first forty-gallon cask is full. For the next ten days or so it will ferment vigorously: every morning an eruption of yeast the size of a cauliflower will have to be knocked off the open bung-hole and the contents topped up. Then a bung will be put in lightly, over a bit of sacking, so that the brew can still expand but the wine-fly cannot get in. Finally the cask will be sealed down tight and left for three or four months to mature.

The cider is about eight per cent alcohol, as strong as table wine. I can feel it going to work. Now Jasper is off on to perry, which he also makes, from pears, and which he claims has an extraordinary effect on women.

'Now there's a queer thing. A lot of ladies don't go for cider. They say, "Cor – that's a bit bread-and-cheesy. That'll cut your throat" – but when we've got a cask of perry on, it fetches 'em from miles.'

No wonder he does a brisk trade in cider at £3 a gallon and perry at £4. Outside, although it is still full daylight, thick fog seems to have closed in. Or has it? I consult my companion. He agrees that fog has descended. Perhaps we had better be going. But there is time for another sup – and as we leave, Jasper's voice comes after me: 'This is cider as it is, and was, and should be. Three pints of this'll put you on your beam ends ...'

Suddenly he veers to the subject of plums and plum jerkum, brewed in the same way as cider and perry. Maybe it is his own brew or the press of visitors that is making him double, treble, quadruple his negatives.

'Trouble with plums,' he says as we pull away, 'there ain't the trade there used to be. I could have picked five or six tons of the buggers this year, but most of 'em rotted, because people don't want plums for jam nor bugger-all no more ...'

❧

Killer in the fields

Once again, myxomatosis has done its fell work. By midsummer our hedges were alive with rabbits, but now there is scarcely one left. As usual, the disease broke out in August, and ever since then the fields have been dotted with moribund victims hopping hopelessly towards their doom.

Horrible as it must be to suffer, myxomatosis is also horrible to see. The rabbits' eyes and noses swell up, oozing pus, and they rapidly lose weight. Becoming blind and debilitated, they blunder into fences and bramble bushes with the inevitable result that they are caught by dogs. When this happens, the only humane thing to do – unpleasant as it seems – is to knock them on the head.

165

If you have dogs with a retrieving instinct, you are then faced with the problem of disposing of the corpse. This is not as easy as it sounds, for my Labradors, having brought a rabbit to me, naturally think that it should be taken home for the pot, and if I try to jettison it privily in a thicket or patch of nettles, they dutifully fish it out again.

The other day, hoping to forestall the usual response, I went so far as to push a body well down a hole and bury it, but one of the dogs dug it out with enormous labour and proudly bore it after me.

Myxomatosis came originally from Uruguay and Brazil, where it is endemic. When it first appeared here during the early 1950s (deliberately introduced, many people claim), attempts were made to contain it within the original area, as attempts would be made to contain an outbreak of rabies.

These, however, soon failed and it tore through the whole country, to the great relief of farmers who, until then, had been severely harassed by the rabbits' depredations.

With its first sweep, it cut down ninety-nine per cent of the population but, after each successive epidemic, a few more survivors seemed to escape. At first it was thought that, by moving out of their traditional burrows and living above ground, the lucky ones had managed to avoid the fleas which transmit the virus. Then it was discovered that the survivors had managed to develop a resistance to the infection, and that an immune female could confer temporary immunity on her young.

Thus a few come through each plague and start to breed again, and in some areas the disease seems to break out again every fourth or fifth year. Even so, numbers have never recovered to anything like their former levels.

The animals most immediately affected by the first mass slaughter were foxes, which until then had lived largely on rabbit. Deprived at a stroke of their major food source, they adapted by concentrating more on mice and beetles. Humans, though less drastically inconvenienced, were also forced to change their habits, since rabbit had for centuries been a staple of country people.

Once you have seen what the disease does to a living creature, you do not feel like eating rabbit at all. Even though it is easy enough to tell a sound animal from a sick one, the mere existence of myxomatosis has certainly put off the great majority of potential consumers, ourselves among them.

Earlier this year, surprised to see local rabbits selling at £1 apiece in a butcher's shop, I mastered my inhibitions and shot and skinned a young one for the pot.

Made into a pie, with onions, green peppers and hard-boiled eggs, it was perfectly delicious. But now that the disease has come back, I fancy that it will be some time before I try another.

What got into the eggs?

Another of the small mysteries that add spice to life in the country seems at last to have resolved itself. This conundrum concerned our eggs, which are, in the most literal sense of the words, free range.

Though confined to a barn at night to protect them from foxes, our chickens forage wherever they like during the day. Farmyard, muck-heap, field, orchard, spinney, wood – everything is open to them except the kitchen garden, and they dine sumptuously on a mixture of household scraps, patent pellets, wheat and whatever vegetable or animal extras they pick up in the course of their daily travels.

Such a diet should produce splendid eggs – and so, until recently, it did. Half-dozens, attractively visible in polythene bags, vanished like smoke from the produce table at fête and coffee morning, and friends on whom we lavished others were loud in their praise. 'Like eggs *used* to taste,' they said.

Then things began to change. Was there a slight coolness, the faintest lack of enthusiasm, when we offered another bowlful? We ourselves started to notice something amiss. Every now and then we got an egg that tasted distinctly sulphurous.

At first we thought that the offenders were old and had got left behind for a few days in one of the outlying nests. But how old, we asked ourselves, is a shop egg anyway? Ten days? A fortnight? Even our most decrepit specimens could not have been around for more than a week. I kept thinking of a line in one of the Western Brothers' patter songs, from days of rationing:

'Don't look at the date on your one Polish egg . . .
Play the game, chaps, play the game.'

Comparative tests soon ruled out antiquity as a possible cause of trouble. Even eggs which we positively knew to be only hours old had the same rebarbative flavour. What was worse, one rotter seemed to permeate an entire omelette or sponge cake and render the whole thing, if not inedible, at least distinctly unpalatable.

We changed the chickens' pellets, then their corn (although they had been getting perfectly plain wheat). We gave them fresh water every few minutes. When none of these innovations produced any effect, our suspicions fell on particular birds, one or two of which, we thought, might have had some physical peculiarity that made their produce tainted; but, although we tried to identify the long eggs, the big ones or the brown ones as the culprits, we could not pin the trouble down.

Enlightenment came suddenly from a sister-in-law who read a magazine article by a man who had once been a professional poultry-keeper. The one thing that had nearly done for him, he recalled, was wild garlic.

Of course! The woods round us are full of the stuff, and its murky, sullen flavour is exactly what we were tasting in the eggs. The garlic has long since died back for the winter, so I imagine that the chickens were scratching out bulbs and eating them. But now – praise be – I can only assume that the birds have polished off all the garlic within reach, for the eggs have suddenly reverted to their original state of excellence and we feel free once more to give them away.

A reader in Hertfordshire, accurately scenting the fact that I have not read *every word* of Thomas Hardy, points out that closer acquaintance with *Tess of the D'Urbervilles* would have given me a clue to the nature of the mystery. Sure enough, there in *Tess* is a scene that rings a bell:

> Dairyman Crick was discovered stamping about the house. He had received a letter, in which a customer had complained that the butter had a twang. 'And begad, so't have!' said the dairyman, who held in his left hand a wooden slice on which a lump of butter was stuck. 'Yes – taste for yourself! . . . Tis garlic! . . . And I thought there wasn't a blade left in that mead . . . We must overhaul that mead . . . this mustn't continny!'

Arming themselves with 'old pointed knives', Crick and his companions, including Tess, form a line and creep slowly back and forth across the field, a strip at a time, digging out every shoot and bulb they can descry. Evidently their efforts are successful, for we hear no more about the problem – or at least, the author seems to become distracted from it by the charms of Tess herself.

I doubt, however, if Crick's method would work for us. Even if we managed to muster a latterday team of garlic-hunters, we should have our work cut out, for although there may be a few plants in our fields, most of them are growing in the wood, which is on a hill with a slope of one-in-three, and for acre after acre the ground is literally full of them – so much so that in spring the whole forest floor sprouts into a waving, dark-green carpet.

I have a vision of the volunteers, urged on by cries of 'Begad!' and 'Tis garlic!', laying waste one small patch but then rebelling against the impossibility of their task. I fear that in this respect we shall have to give nature best. For the moment, thank goodness, the twang has gone from the eggs; if it returns, the only practicable solution will be to confine the chickens to garlic-free areas.

DECEMBER

Wanted – a pied piper

It is not very nice to be invaded suddenly by rats. If you live in the middle of arable land, as we used to, you positively expect to be overrun soon after the harvest is finished: with food and shelter both gone, the vermin naturally draw in to farm buildings. In grassland there is no such violent seasonal change to make them shift their quarters. Nevertheless, during the past few days they have arrived with a vengeance.

Of the many features that make rats unattractive, not the least is the filthiness of their habits. They eat anything they can get hold of, including other animals that are still alive but incapacitated, and each others' dead bodies, and they excrete all over the place, fouling their own living areas with reckless abandon. The choking, acrid smell which they create makes it easy to believe that in the Middle Ages black rats spread bubonic plague and to this day *Rattus norvegicus* carries jaundice.

Contemporary accounts give a vivid idea of how rats exasperated earlier generations. 'Of all manner of vermin Cornish houses are most pestered with rats,' wrote Richard Carew in his *Survey of Cornwall*, published in 1602. He described them as 'a brood very hurtful for devouring of meat, clothes and writings by day, and alike cumbersome through their crying and rattling, while they dance their gallop galliards in the roof at night.'

Clearly things were worse then than now. As far as I know, we do not yet have rats in the house (although the other morning a fine specimen of a mouse ran between my bare feet as I stood shaving in the bathroom) and certainly no deathless prose has yet been consumed by rodents. But it is bad enough to have the farm buildings infested.

To the *Oxford Dictionary of Natural History* rats are 'perhaps the most successful of all mammalian families' – a zoologist's way of saying that they are phenomenal survivors. They are certainly hyperactive, and another characteristic which makes them so unpleasant is their combination of frantic energy and furtiveness. Once they are established in a stack of bales, there is continual squeaking, rustling and burrowing about, and if all is quiet outside, scouts soon start venturing forth, even in full daylight; but never for a second, it seems, do any of them keep still. This makes them fleeting targets and difficult to shoot.

They also have astonishing powers of penetration, invading areas which look far beyond their reach. They climb with squirrel-like agility and force their way through apparently impregnable defences. The havoc they can cause beneath concrete floors, by tunnelling and hollowing out the subsoil, is amazing.

The obvious way of dealing with an infestation is to call in the local pest officer – but he would put down poisoned bait, and in a farmyard patrolled by chickens and dogs the distribution of poison is a risky business. Even if it is laid with care, in places inaccessible to other creatures, it is perfectly possible that the dogs will catch and eat a rat rendered lethargic by dope.

At the moment I am campaigning with traps, set in specially made tunnels and baited with various delicacies. So far, I must admit, I have not had much luck, the total bag being one; but I intend to persevere and hope that by scrupulously removing all other food I shall gradually force the rats to address themselves to my offerings. In the meantime, I should be delighted to hear of any latterday Pied Piper who would come and charm them away.

Omnivorous quadrupeds

Rats are truly omnivorous, but one would not normally say the same of horses, yet I am beginning to believe that the two old-stagers which we have at the moment really would eat anything set before them.

Somehow, greed seems less reprehensible in animals than in human beings. When once our donkey got at the chicken food and was found horizontal, unable to do more than twitch his toes, the fact that he had eaten himself within inches of extinction seemed hilarious rather than disgusting.

In the same way, a gluttonous Garron pony which I knew in the Highlands delighted everyone with his passion for sandwiches. In order to catch him in the mornings and avoid, as he put it, 'being given the heels', his ghillie usually had to sacrifice most of his piece or picnic lunch; and, although the horse would put away ham or marmite with relish, he made no secret of his preference for strawberry jam.

All the same, there are limits, and I felt we had reached one this week when both our horses simultaneously leaned over the fence of the garden and made away with the vegetables I had just picked for dinner. One went off with a roll of chard leaves sticking sideways out of his mouth like a cigar, the other with a whole bunch of carrots dangling by their stalks like icicles of frozen beard. Needless to say, the flapping movement of the carrots struck him as highly dangerous and he took off for two ritual circuits of the field, flat out.

Since this animal has already eaten all the broccoli plants within reach and since, one summer evening, I saw his companion tidy up the day's crop of courgettes which I had been foolish enough to leave on the path, neither is entirely popular – and the two put me more and more in mind of the goat which drove that splendid mariner Joshua Slocum to distraction during his circumnavigation at the end of the last century.

In his classic *Sailing Alone Around the World*, Slocum described how the goat, given him on St Helena, proved so dreadfully voracious that he abandoned it in disgust on his next stepping-stone north, Ascension Island. By then it had eaten his shoes, a good deal of the rigging and his chart of the West Indies, and he gave a real cry from the heart when he recorded: 'Alas, there was not a rope in the sloop proof against that goat's awful teeth.'

Nature's alarm signals

'The cocks are on,' my companion observed. In another context, I reflected, the remark could have referred to plumbing or to the innards of a ship; but, in fact, I and a gamekeeper were standing quietly in a wood, listening to pheasant alarm calls ricocheting from the other side of the valley.

For a few minutes the noise remained more or less stationary. Two birds were chiping (as the keeper called it), a few yards apart, warning that some predator was on the move. At first we thought it might be a stoat or cat, but then suddenly another cock started, some 200 yards to the left, and we knew from the speed at which the centre of disturbance had shifted that the marauder must be a fox.

The interpretation of alarm calls is a fascinating art, which one gradually learns from experience. Some species of bird give much more definite information than others. A jay, for instance, screams out the same harsh warning at any creature that has frightened him, be it man, owl, hawk, fox or dog. A blackbird, on the other hand, has two quite different calls to give early warning of possible ground or air attack: for hawks or owls he flies away with a shrill, chattering screech, whereas for a stoat, weasel, fox or cat he holds his position and gives off a low *tuk, tuk, tuk*. If you hear a wren whirring like an alarm clock, you can be sure that there is something nasty near it on the ground. Pheasants are less discriminating, and only the intensity of their reaction gives an idea of the nature of the threat. If they merely begin chiping, it is a general indication of danger but, if they start taking off – hens with high-pitched squeaks, cocks with rattling calls – they are probably being flushed by the immediate menace of a fox or dog.

Such signs of agitation are not to be confused, of course, with the routine chorus which signals the ascent to roost every evening – and for me no sound is more evocative of the English winter than the staccato cries that echo through the woods as the frost bites, the light dies, and the cocks go aloft for the night.

Darkness often brings another phenomenon whose significance I do not understand. Sometimes on a still night there sounds from way beyond the horizon a dull, low-frequency thud: it could be a late blast from some distant quarry or the dying fall of a sonic boom as Concorde comes in over the Atlantic. Whatever it is, the noise is so low that human ears can scarcely pick it up. But every cock pheasant

173

hears it and every one lets fly a retort. For a few seconds the woods ring with an echoing clamour. Is it defiance or mutual reassurance? I never know. But in a few moments it is over and silence settles back on to the trees.

Plum's navigation

Delighted as I always am to hear of some feat of direction-finding performed by an animal or bird, I remain sceptical in the face of the latest claim to come my way. It is said that a hare captured in Poland and released with some others as part of an experiment in France made its way home across 1,200 miles of alien territory only to be shot (and recognized from its metal ear-tag) in Tarnobrzeg, where it had started life.

The Polish weekly *Politika* of course suggested that the hare, being a good socialist, came home because it was disgusted with the French Government, but I wonder whether it could really have managed such a journey. Is it not more likely that someone did a bit of jiggery-pokery with the ear-tags, holding one back from the consignment of hares that went to France and slipping it on to a local animal?

Whatever the answer, I was astonished by the story (which I *know* to be true) of our neighbour's Labrador Plum, who once tried to track him down across the centre of London. He, as it happened, had gone to Norwich for the day; but in the middle of the morning the dog, who had slipped away from home in Notting Hill Gate, arrived unannounced at his master's chambers in the Temple.

It is true that Plum was no stranger to legal precincts and had often been to the Temple before, but he had never gone there on foot, always arriving or leaving in a vehicle. How did he find his way for at least four miles through traffic-choked streets of which he had no direct experience? He could not have followed human scent, for his master had not been near his chambers that day, but had taken a taxi direct to Liverpool Street. Did Plum go straight or did he have to cast about? And what route did he take – Oxford Street and High Holborn? Soho? Hyde Park, Constitution Hill and the Embankment? Alas, we shall never know, for, like the Polish hare, he has taken his secret with him.

That dogs do have some superhuman power of orientation –

whether derived from scent or some form of radar, or a combination of both – has been proved on countless occasions. I remember once staying overnight at a country house and, in the morning, going for a walk round the garden with the owner, preceded by an ancient Golden Retriever, which had long since gone blind. As we walked along a grass path between flowerbeds, the old dog hesitated, gathered himself and suddenly jumped high in the air, landing four or five feet further on. For a moment I thought he had been stung by a wasp or a bee – but then my host produced a touching explanation.

Before the advent of myxomatosis the land had been infested with rabbits and, to keep them out, the garden had been encircled by a fence of wire-netting, which used to cross the path at that point. In the past two years the rabbits had died from the disease and the unsightly fence had been dismantled, but the retriever, having lost his sight in the meantime, never realized that the barrier had gone and, when his other senses told him he had reached the take-off point, he jumped – to the end of his days.

Lily of the valley

Speculation has been raging in the village about the motives and possible future movements of a lone mute swan, which arrived one day on the little lake in the valley. The question was whether or not it had inadvertently trapped itself by landing on a stretch of water too small to allow it to take off again.

Interest was fuelled by the fact that the bird was visible from miles off. From many a vantage point on the hills around it could be seen gliding majestically about the pond, beautifully white and, as the days passed, people began to suggest that Maurice, the local bookmaker, should lay odds on whether it would still be here for Christmas.

Those who thought it was grounded – or, at least, water-bound – favoured some sort of rescue operation. The rival faction (among whom I numbered myself) maintained that it was merely resting and would depart in its own good time: it had, after all, nearly 100 yards of water as a runway and to make a getaway needed only to clear a low bank and sheep fence on take-off. I assumed that, just as an aircraft-carrier needs to establish a certain speed of wind over the deck for the launch and recovery of fighters, so the swan was waiting for a good westerly airstream to come blasting up the valley and give it maximum lift.

Certainly it was not short of food. A swan's normal diet consists mostly of grass and water weeds, but this bird soon found its menu greatly extended by the ministrations of well-wishers, who hurried to bring it bread, corn and – when the idea got about that it needed vitamins – shredded cabbage.

A call to the Wildfowl Trust at Slimbridge suggested that there was no cause for alarm. An expert confirmed that young mute swans wander widely and often spend a few days on some outlying patch of water before returning to their native haunts. Although they do usually take off after a long, flapping paddle or run, they can also launch themselves almost vertically if they have to – witness the recent escape of a bird being treated for lead poisoning, which managed to clear four-foot-high netting with no run at all. The expert further predicted that if hard weather came in and the pond froze, *our* swan would soon push off.

So it proved. With the recent cold snap, the pond iced over and one morning, just as the water began to freeze, the bird took off, half paddling, half skating. Now everyone hopes that it will return, for the view was enormously enhanced by the sight of such a mysterious stranger floating like an exotic lily in the valley.

All four wheels u/s

It was not an ideal site on which to lose propulsion: a track frozen into rock-hard ruts of mud, deep in a wood more than a mile from the nearest village. But still – would this not be an ideal test for the great rescue organization which I had joined earlier in the year?

A brisk walk brought me to a cottage, and from there I telephoned the Great Rescue Organization's breakdown office. A girl began to take my particulars, but soon fetched up on the reef of bureaucracy.

'What road is the vehicle on?'

'It's not on a road. It's in the middle of a wood.'

'What's the wood called?'

'Well – there's no point in my telling you, because it's not marked on the map. But it's on the Blank Estate.' I could tell that this had not gone down too well, so I suggested that I should walk out to the village and meet the rescue driver at the pub there.

'Oh no,' said the girl. 'You can't do that.'

'Why not? It's the only way he'll find me.'

'If you're not with the vehicle, you haven't got a breakdown.'

'I most certainly *have* got a breakdown.'

'Well, I can't do anything about it.'

The supervisor was more helpful and agreed that a recovery truck would meet me at the pub 'within an hour'. I left the cottage and started to walk, but almost at once met the gamekeeper in a Land Rover, so we went back and towed my own jeep up to the village. Thus, after only half an hour, I and my cripple were both outside the Carpenter's Arms.

Time passed. As the light faded, the frost came down hard. A man in a cottage next to the pub saw me loitering and kindly offered a cup of tea. 'Bring your dog in, too,' he said. 'You must both be frozen.'

Thank heavens I decided that Zephyr (a young Labrador with imperfectly functioning control systems) would be happier on board. As I stood in the dusky sitting-room, waiting for my host to boil a kettle, I became aware of movement round my feet and saw that what I had at first taken for a cat was in fact a black rabbit with a white nose. Now Zephyr is mustard on rabbits: had she come in, the animal would have survived about fifteen seconds, and in that time most of the room's furniture and ornaments would have been reduced to matchwood or powder.

Night fell. Two hours after my first call, I rang again. Headquarters assured me that 'a local firm' was on its way. More than another hour passed before a rescue truck at last appeared – and then the driver gave the game away by revealing that he had not been contacted until half an hour after my second summons. Trying to use one of its own vehicles, the GRO had held off for as long as possible before resorting to outside help.

No matter: this driver was an excellent young fellow. Not till he had hoisted the jeep's back wheels on to his towing cradle did we realize that the vehicle was jammed in four-wheel drive. The only thing for it was to disconnect the propellor shaft underneath – a horrible job at the best of times, which he did with bare hands, in ten degrees of frost, without the ghost of a complaint. The fact that his cargo included a dog and a high-velocity rifle disconcerted him not at all.

As we went swaying back to civilization, I reflected that there were two small compensations for my ruined afternoon. One was that I had achieved a small victory over a bureaucrat, and the other that somebody's pet rabbit was still in the land of the living.

A visitor's shots in the dark

The bombardment opened soon after dawn. As I was making coffee, shots began to boom from the head of the valley. I went outside to investigate. Under a clear sky daybreak was coming up early, but still it was half dark and the moon hung high above the hill.

Lack of visibility evidently posed no difficulty to the gunner. *Bang! Bang!* With echoes rolling in all directions, it was impossible to pinpoint the origin of the shots, but they seemed to be coming from the wood in which the local shoot has its pheasant release pen, and after five doubles and as many singles in rapid succession I decided some poacher must be making hay among the young birds.

Early as it was, I thought I had better ring the man who runs the shoot.

'Don't worry,' he said. 'It's only a bloke from one of the holiday cottages. He asked if he could try out a new gun, and I gave him permission.'

'Well – all I can say is that he's blazing away like a lunatic. There he goes again. . . . What the hell can he be shooting *at?*'

'Rabbits, I expect.'

'But there aren't that many rabbits.'

'Pigeons, then . . .'

I rang off and sat down to work. But fresh salvoes kept roaring out – two doubles, three. Try as I might to ignore the noise, I could not help counting the shots – and by the time the explosions petered out, the total was between sixty and seventy. I imagined the marksman staggering home to breakfast, barrels smoking, barely able to walk beneath the weight of his bag.

That evening the shoot manager came round to apologize.

'It didn't worry me,' I said. 'But I'd love to know how he did. What did he get?'

'Oh – nothing,' came the answer. 'He never touched a feather.'

A fruitful day in the orchard

It goes against the grain to cut down fruit trees. Even if they have reached the end of their useful lives, you know that somebody carefully planted them, however long ago; the planter and his successors looked after them, and countless people have enjoyed the produce over the seasons.

Shades of Chekhov hovered as I went into action against some superannuated apple trees. Was I a latterday version of Lopakhin, the jumped-up peasant turned property speculator who in *The Cherry Orchard* plans to build holiday cottages once he has had the old trees cleared away? But as I got going, my attitude became more robust. I had no intention of selling the land for cottages. My plan from the outset was to start a new orchard on a fresh piece of ground and plant more trees than I cut down. This I have now done, replacing in the ratio of two to one. Admittedly one of the saplings – a Bramley – was ruined by a rabbit eating its bark before I could fit it with defensive wire; but that tree has itself been replaced and the rabbit is in the deep-freeze, so I reckon that overall I have made a sizable improvement to the property.

Whiter than the morning sky

It is good to be past the winter solstice – the shortest day of the year – for our house stands on the north slope of a hill and in the depths of winter the sun does not come on us until after midday. It is annoying still to be in shadow while the village basks in sunshine on the other side of the valley – although we do have the compensation of remaining in the sun for the whole of the afternoon.

Unlike the arrival of winter and summer time, the solstice provokes no argument in our household: the sooner it is gone, the better. Those other milestones in the calendar, by contrast, always cause commotion. No matter how often winter and summer time come round, I can never decide whether the clocks should go forward or back; and when, after protracted debate, we decide on one or the other, we are almost always wrong – like the American friend who, convinced that his time was six hours ahead of ours, once telephoned me at 3.30 am.

Now in the winter, when I am out of doors at dawn or dusk, I often reflect on the question of whether there is any intrinsic difference between morning and evening light. I am haunted by Chatterton's magical phrase 'Whiter than the morning sky'.

I am half persuaded that a difference does exist. But I can never be sure that the apparent variations are not merely the product of built-in knowledge. Because you already know more or less what time it is and have your compass bearings, you automatically distinguish between a fiery dawn and a blazing sunset. Yet if you woke up in hospital after a spell of unconsciousness, and knew neither the time of day nor east and west, would you be able to tell from the sky whether it was morning or evening? I doubt it – and I am driven to the reluctant conclusion that even though Chatterton's line raises echoes that will ring in my mind for ever, it really means nothing at all.

Sett and match to badgers

The best Christmas news to have come my way so far is the Government's announcement that it is to call off its persecution of badgers. Even after large-scale gassing and years of argument, there is still very little agreement about whether or not badgers spread bovine tuberculosis, and the official closure of the extermination campaign amounts to a tacit admission that the case against them is not proven.

One fact, however, is obvious to anybody who lives in badger territory. This is that they very soon re-colonize any area from which their predecessors have been cleared. Our valley was the scene of one of the Ministry of Agriculture's early extermination campaigns, but now it is well stocked again, with sets freshly worked and broad, beaten trails running through the woods.

From this it follows that our surviving badgers, if they are carrying tuberculosis, must have brought it with them into this valley from wherever they originated. In other words, to wipe out the population in any particular area merely increases the chances of the disease moving from one community to another.

Not the least attraction of badgers is their secretive nature. Because they live (and, if they are gassed, die) underground and have nocturnal habits, it is very hard to tell how large the population may be. A neighbouring farmer, whose judgement I respect in other matters, assured me the other day that there used to be 5,000 badgers in our valley; but the figure seemed utterly unrealistic, and from my own observations I doubt whether there were ever more than a tenth as many.

Now there may be no more than 100 and, although evidence of their presence is everywhere, I have yet to set eyes on one. The only time I deliberately set out to look for them, taking along a German friend, we received a surprise. Scarcely had we settled to watch, above some extensive earthworks on a wooded hillside, when a loud rumble sounded almost under our feet. I nudged Hans to make sure he had his camera ready, and out shot not a badger but a large dog fox, which erupted into the evening air about ten feet away. For a German, who expects every fox to be rabid and bent on attack, it was an unsettling moment.

Trees that walk away

The past week has been a harassing one for the landowners who grow Christmas trees. For one thing trees have a sinister habit of moving off out of the woods during the night, as it were under their own power; and for another, the influx of foreign trees from Belgium and the Netherlands, which everyone here hoped would have been damned by adverse exchange rates, has continued unabated.

Continental trees first came in on a big scale in 1980 and in that year, coincidentally, was formed the British Christmas Tree Growers' Association, which now has 300 members and campaigns to get people to buy home stock.

The trade is lucrative but tricky. As one grower put it, 'Few things are more worthless than a cut Christmas tree on 26 December.' But by then between four and five million trees will have been sold, probably a third of them from abroad. The favourite species by far is still Norway spruce, and the trend seems to be towards taller trees, six or eight feet high (at about £1.20 a foot retail).

The art of the grower is to keep his outlets stocked up without cutting more than he need. Anything left growing can be kept in shape by a bit of careful pruning and take its chance next year. If anyone wants a tip about how to stop the needles falling – much the best thing is to stand the tree in a bucket of stones topped up with water.

Pachydermatous Radio Duff

To my great delight I have just heard that Radio Duff is alive and well and on the air. The output of the station could hardly be called entertaining, consisting as it does of a two-tone signal, endlessly repeated – but it is certainly of interest to those who listen out for it.

Radio Duff, it must be explained, is a Greater One-Horned Rhino. He lives in the agreeable surroundings of the Royal Chitwan National Park, in the south of Nepal. Being rather short-sighted, like all his kin, he sees nothing in the stunning array of Himalayan peaks which command his northern horizon, but I am sure he appreciates the comforts of the lush, sub-tropical jungle and grassland that are his home.

It was there, almost a year ago, that I shot him in the backside with an anaesthetic dart. To forestall complaints about cruelty, I should explain that I did this at the behest of Dr Hemanta Mishra, one of Nepal's leading conservation officers, who is conducting a programme of research into rhino habits.

The missile was not one by which you or I would care to be penetrated – about eight inches long overall with a needle the length and diameter of a four-inch nail. Even the rhino found it less than pleasant experience: he took off with a snort and cantered a couple of hundred yards, smashing down the undergrowth like a runaway tank.

When the immobilizing drug took effect, he began to sway back and forth on his feet, and then lay down. As soon as he was safely unconscious, we dismounted from our elephants to take measurements and fit his radio collar.

It was very odd to be able to approach and touch so huge and potentially dangerous an animal. To describe him as an incredible hulk would be to do him less than justice. There was something positively prehistoric about the thickness of his creased and folded skin: punching it with my fist on his shoulder, I could feel that flesh lay deep beneath the armour – but only just.

The great beast had gone down on his front with his head tilted to the left. When Dr Mishra's assistant wanted to measure the long canine tooth on the left-hand side of his mouth, I said, 'I'll roll his head over for you.' 'I don't think you will,' came the reply – and I soon found out why. It took three of us to turn probably three-quarters of a ton of bone and muscle from one side to the other.

Within twenty minutes our new transmitter was ready to go, with a miniature radio fitted to a heavy-duty nylon band round his neck. In my honour he was named Radio Duff.

'All aboard!' Dr Mishra called, and we scrambled back to the safety of our elephants before he administered the antidote. In four or five minutes the rhino came to, tottered a few steps and then walked firmly off, already sending out his signal.

Since then, by broadcasting continuous news of his movements – which speed up no end when the fires of lust consume him – he has contributed a good deal to the study in hand; and at this time of year particularly I like to think of him going about his business under the winter sun, with the midday temperature at a comfortable 75°F and the eternal snows of Annapurna gleaming white on the horizon. There is something rather satisfactory about the fact that one's representative and namesake in such an exotic setting should be a two-ton radio pachyderm.